THE FOUR REALMS

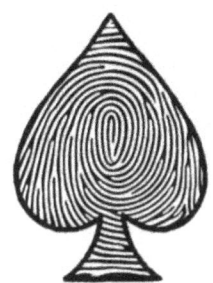 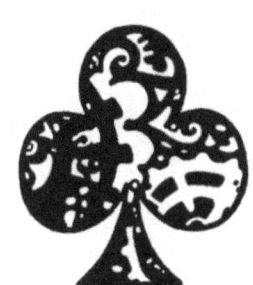 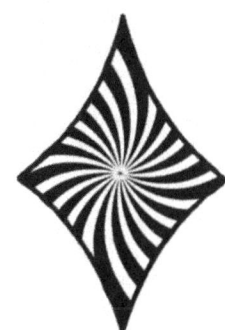 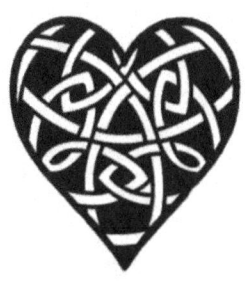

A COLORING BOOK FOR ADULTS BY

LISA MITROKHIN

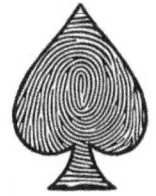  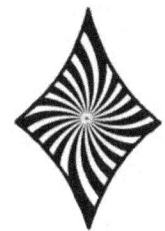 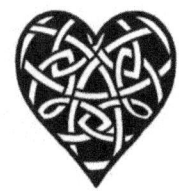

THIS BOOK IS DEDICATED TO

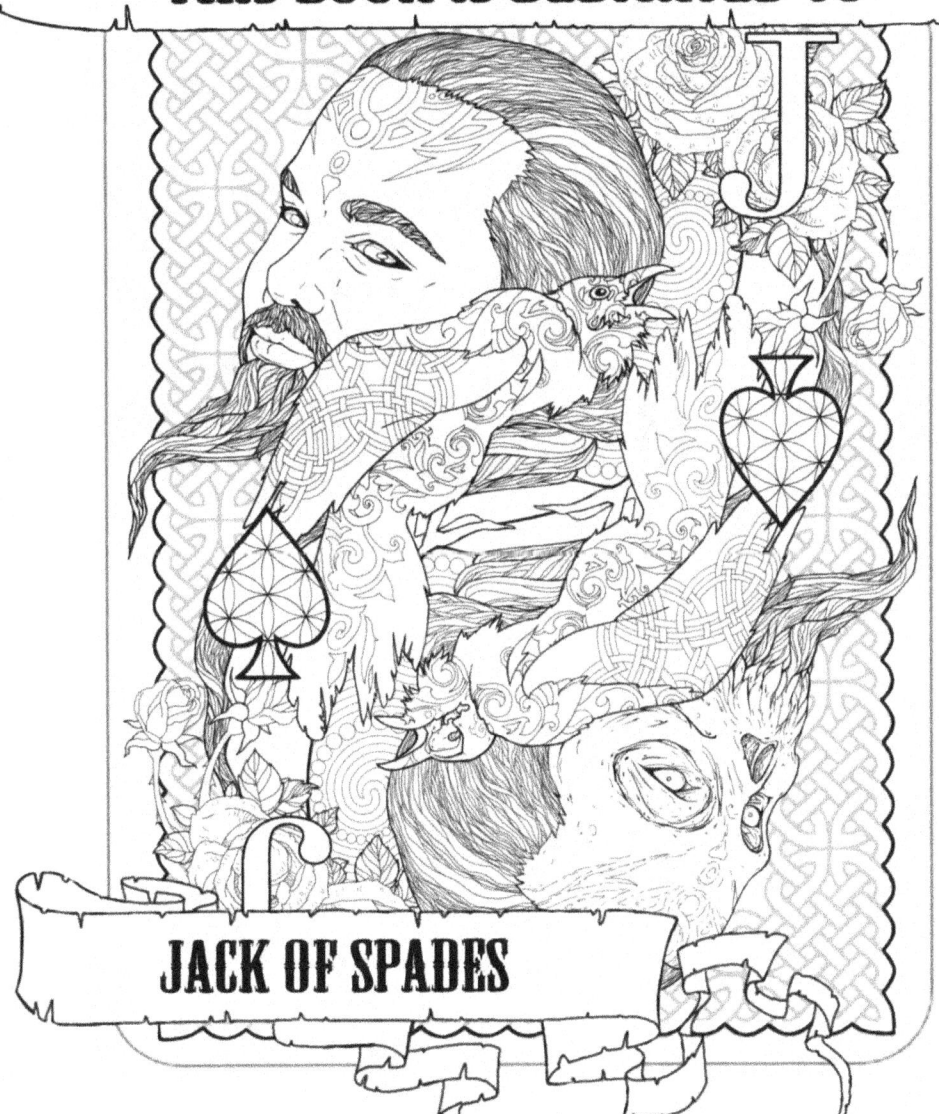

JACK OF SPADES

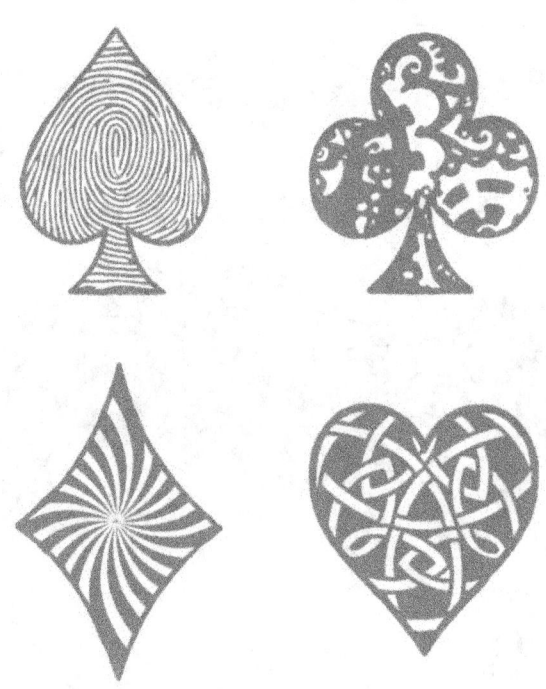

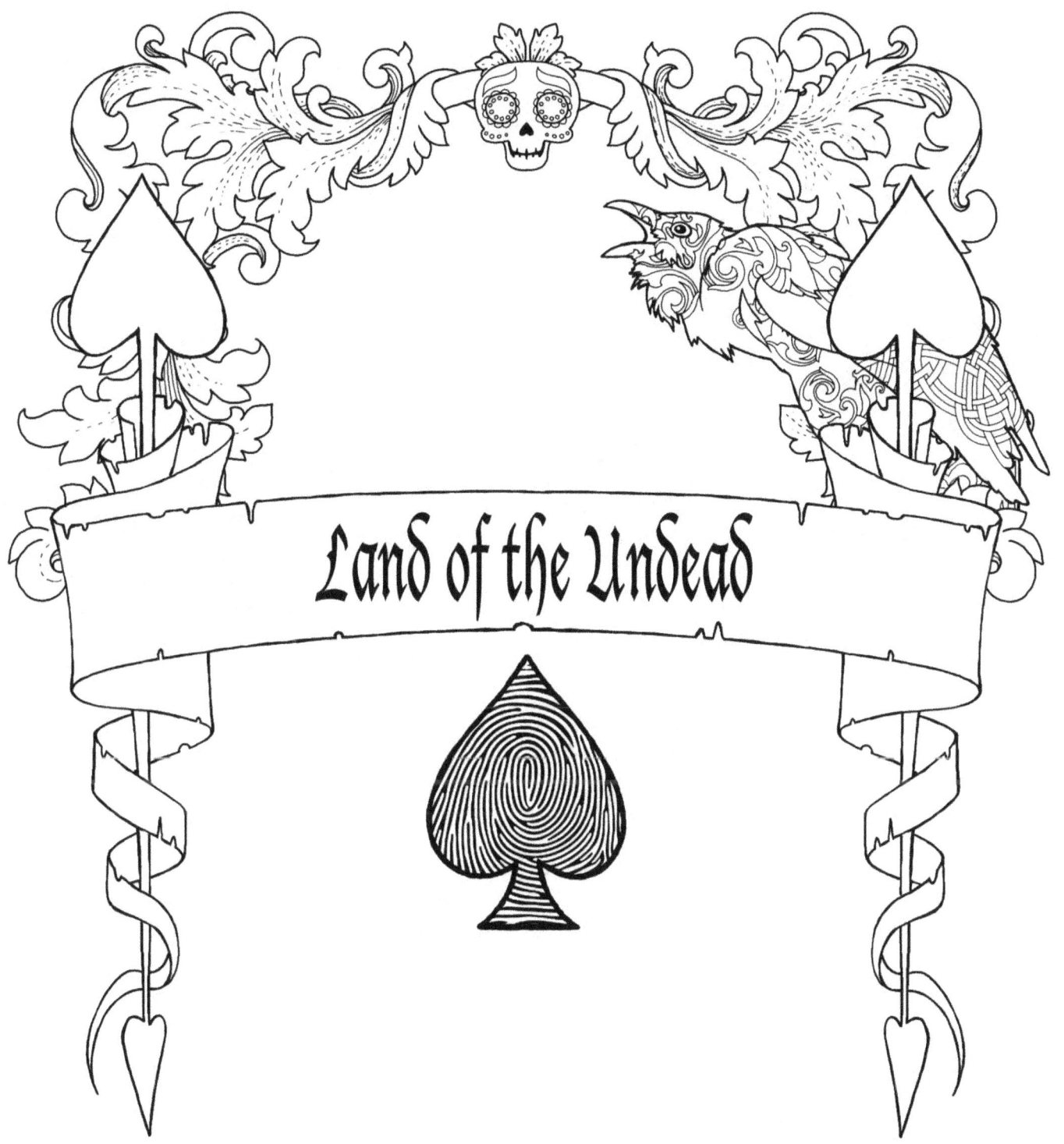

Land of the Undead

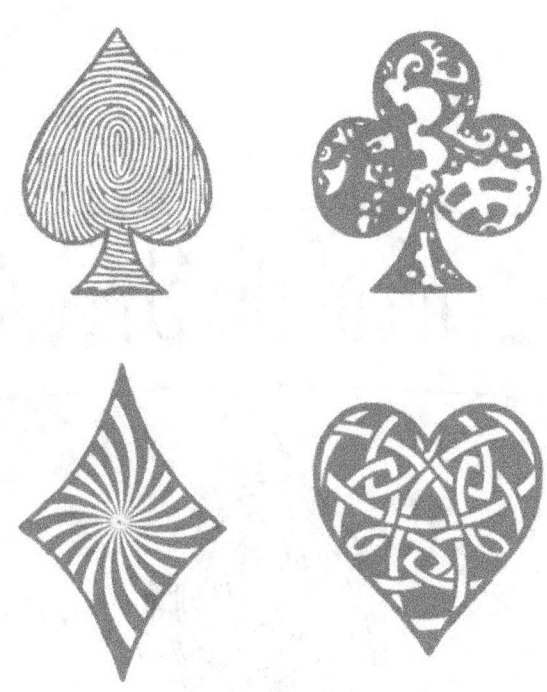

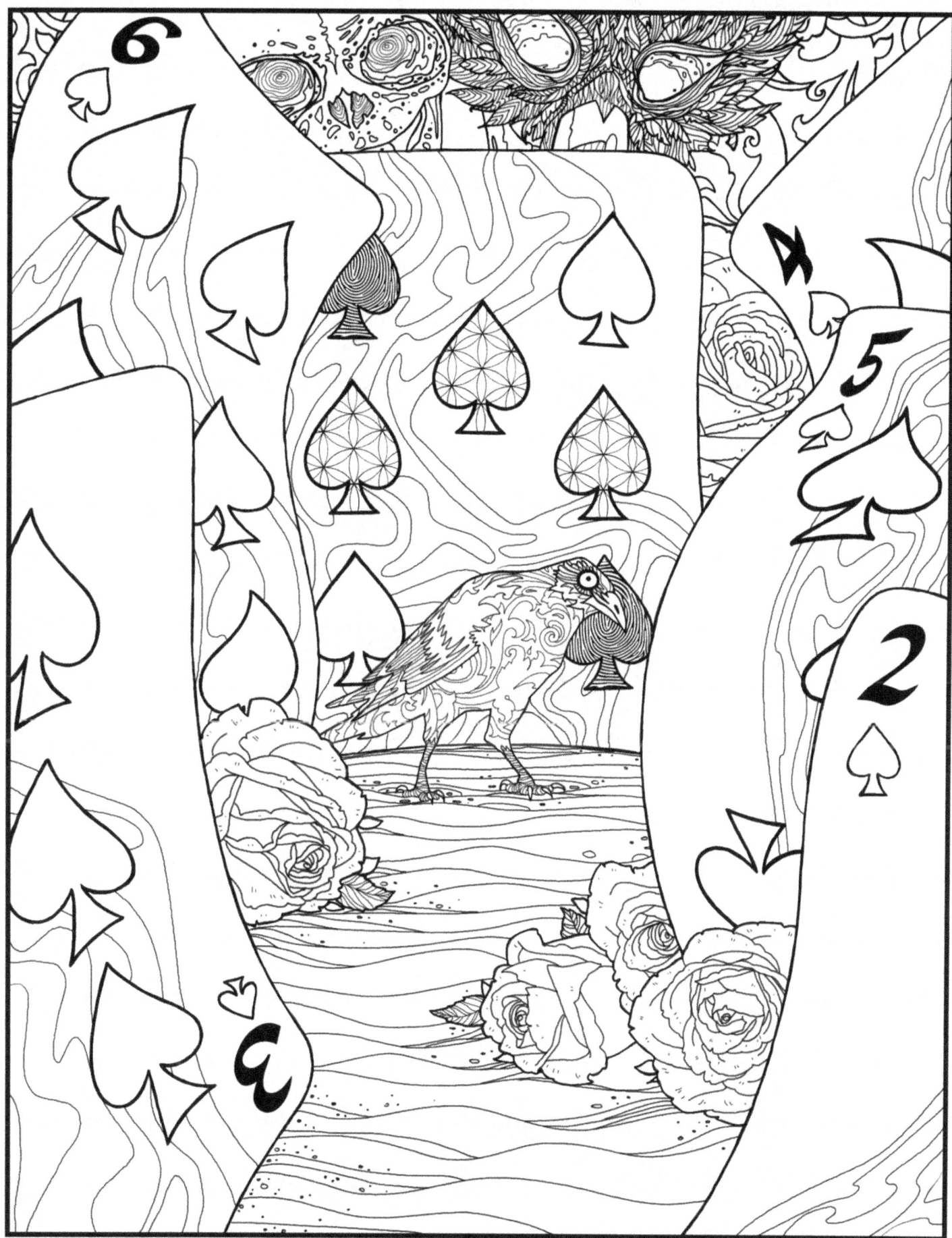

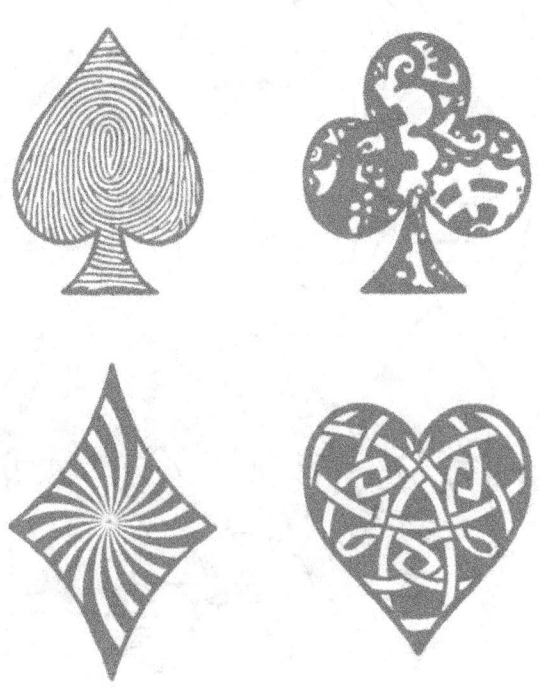

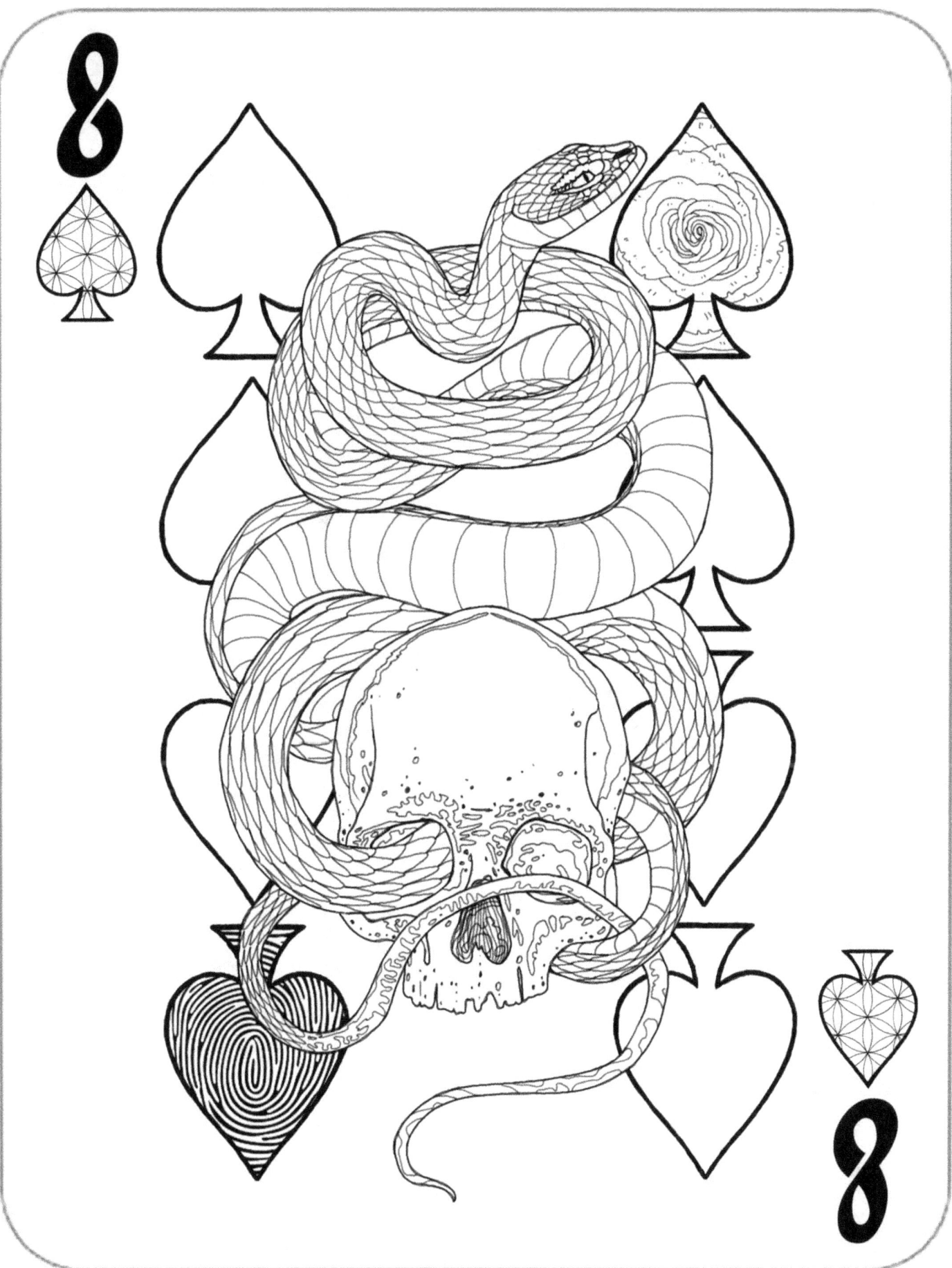

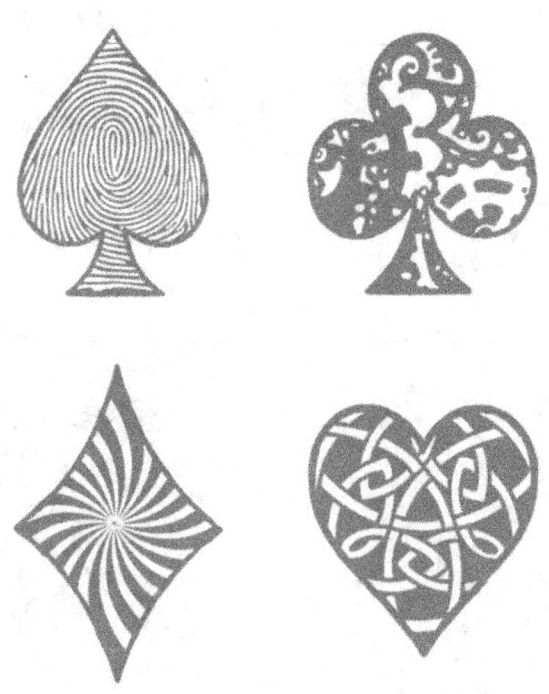

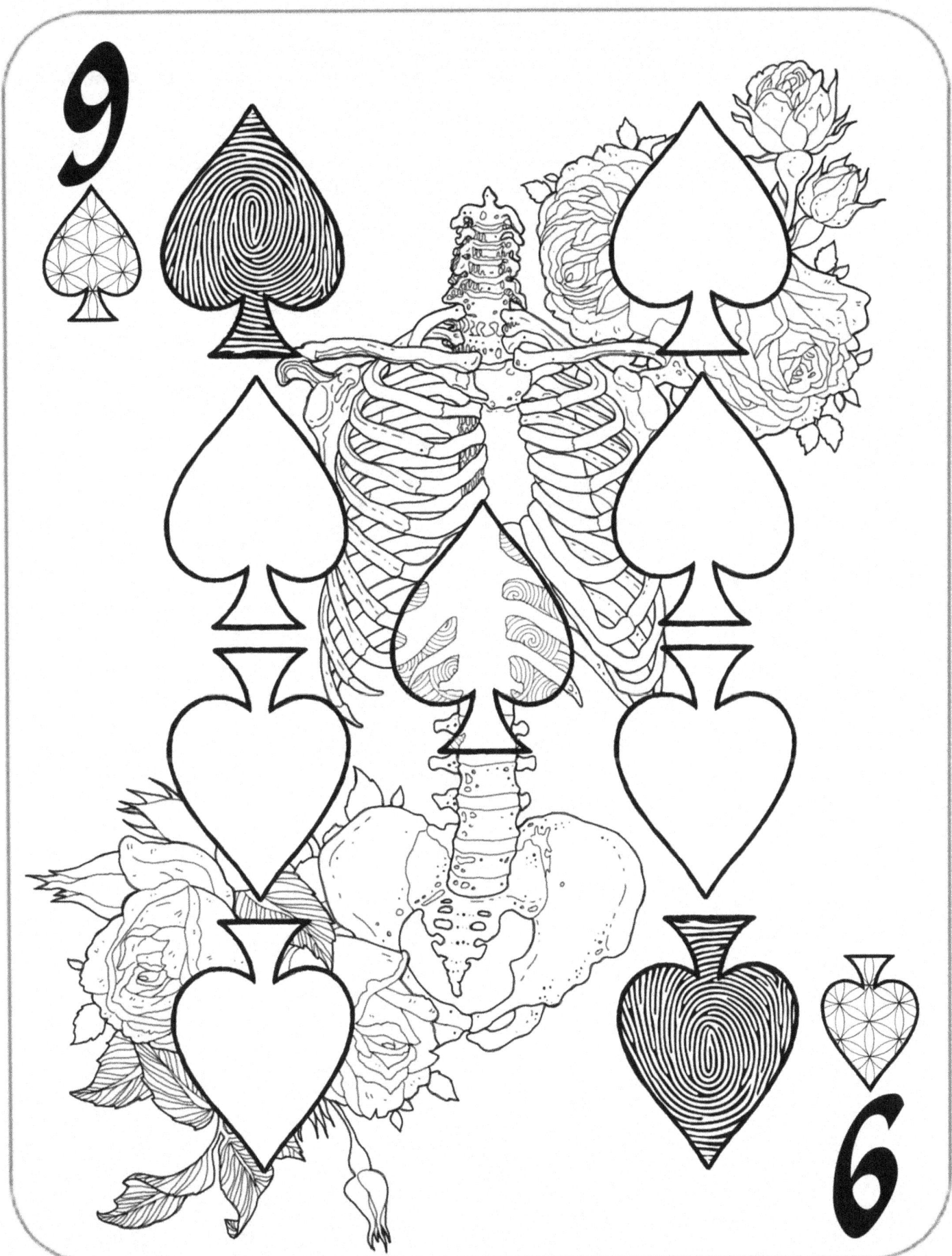

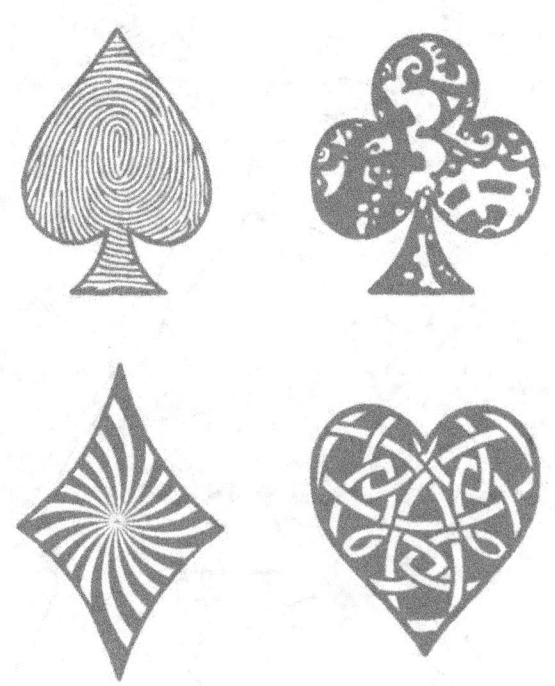

© Lisa Mitrokhin

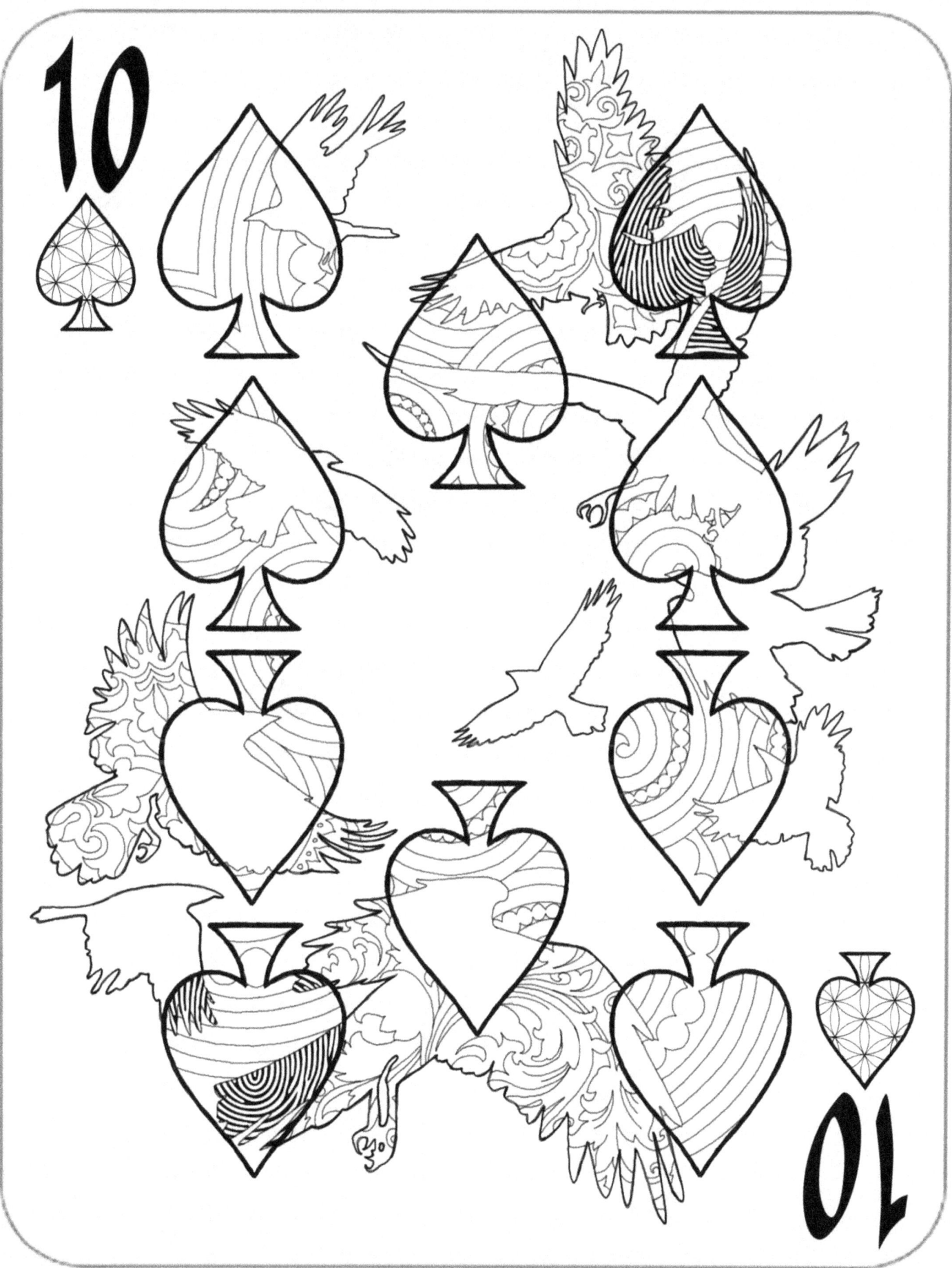

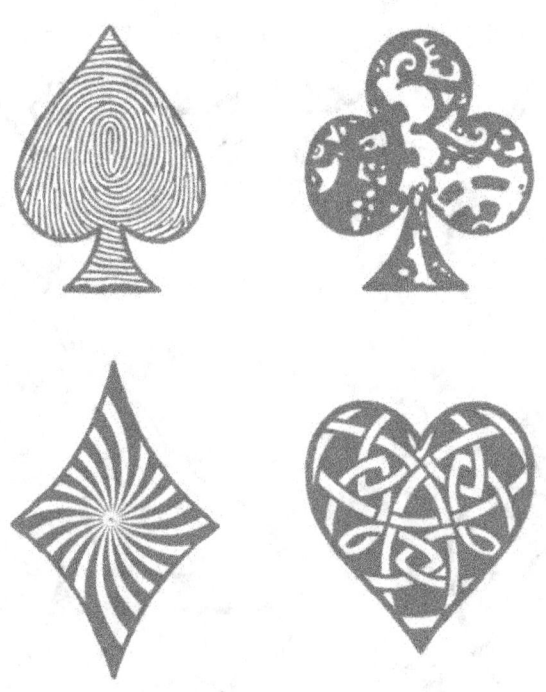

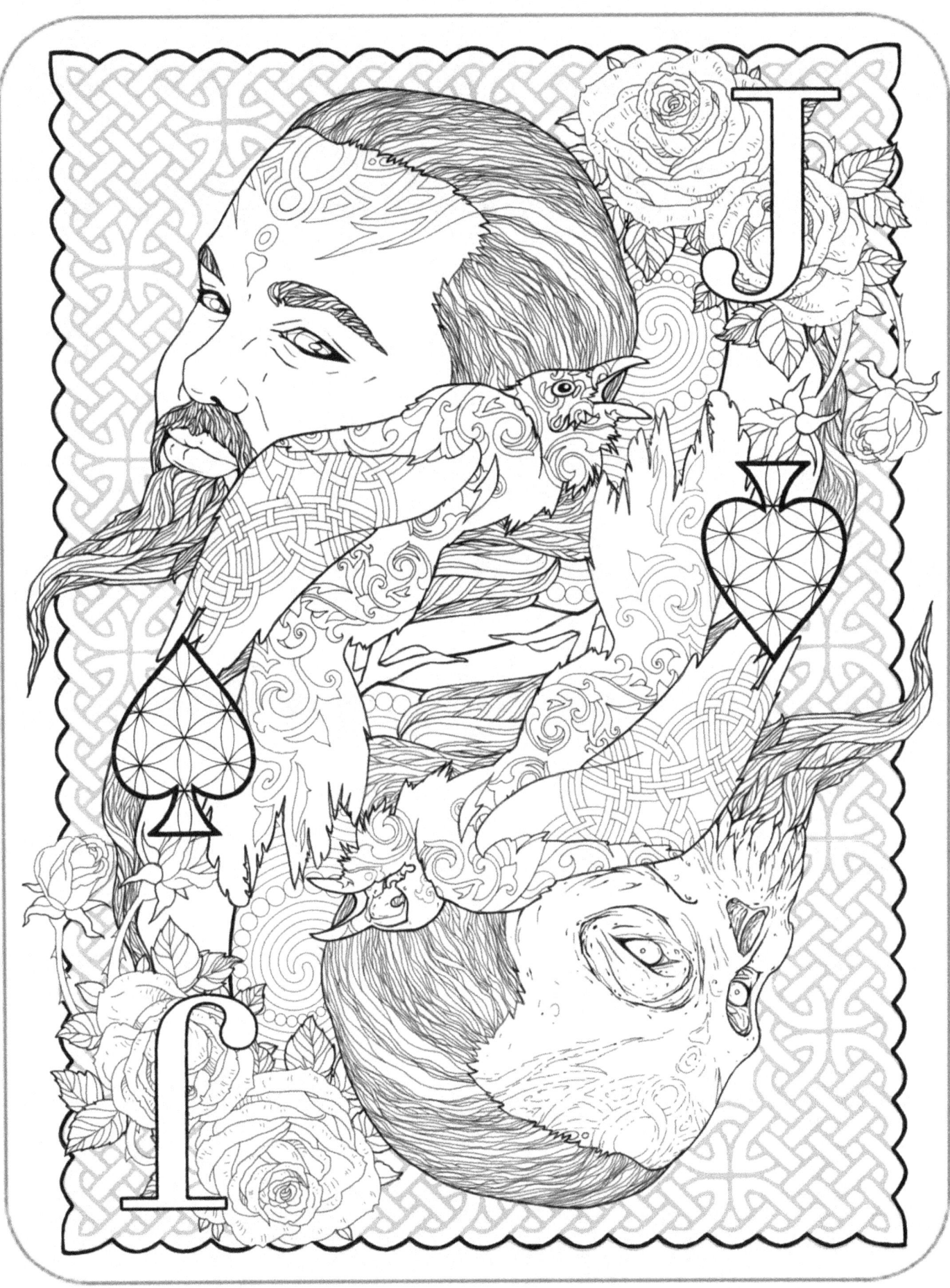

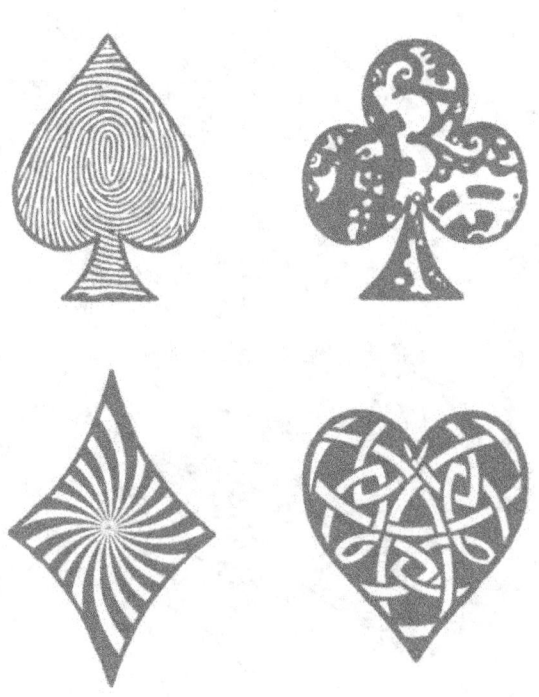

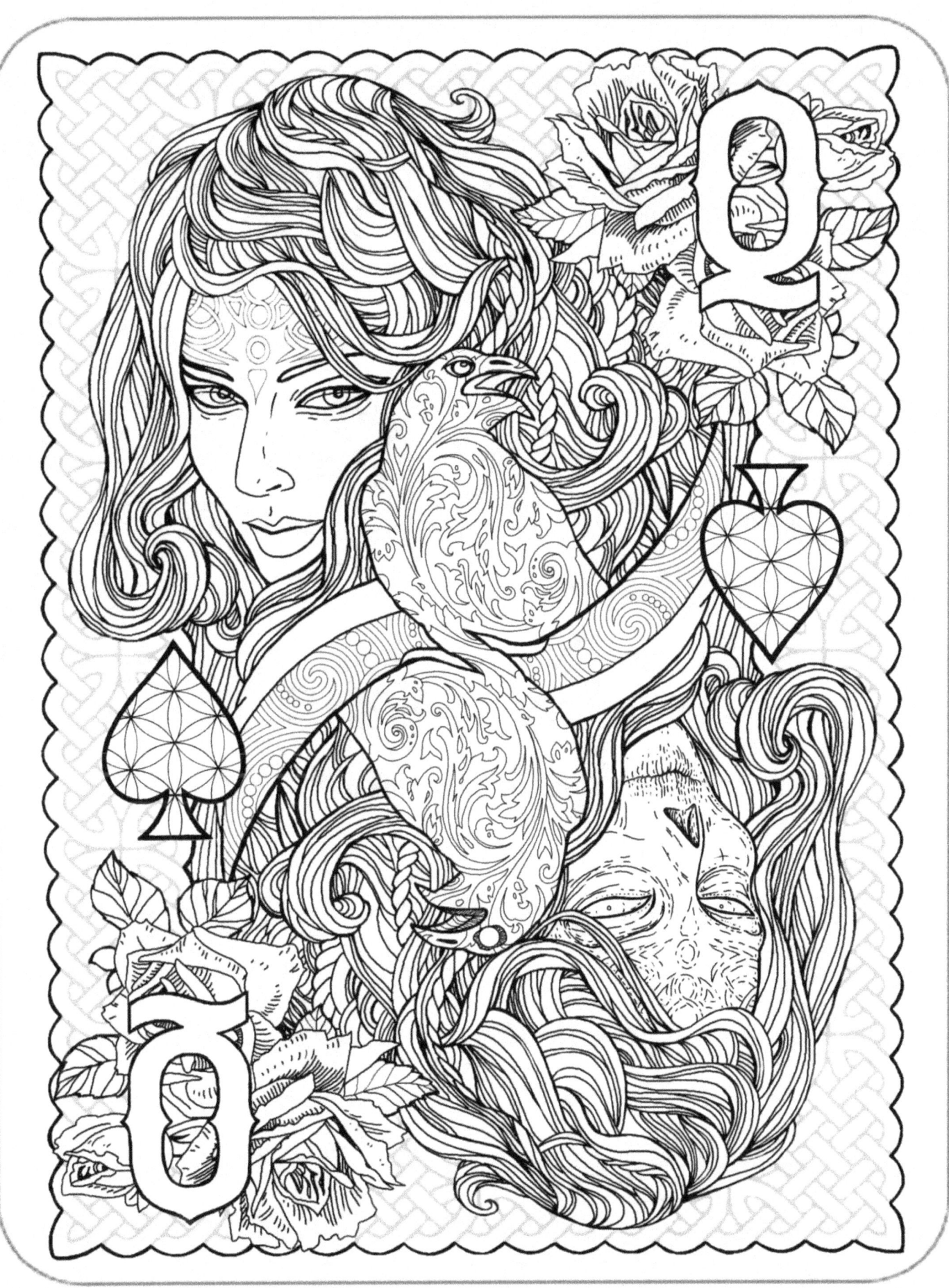

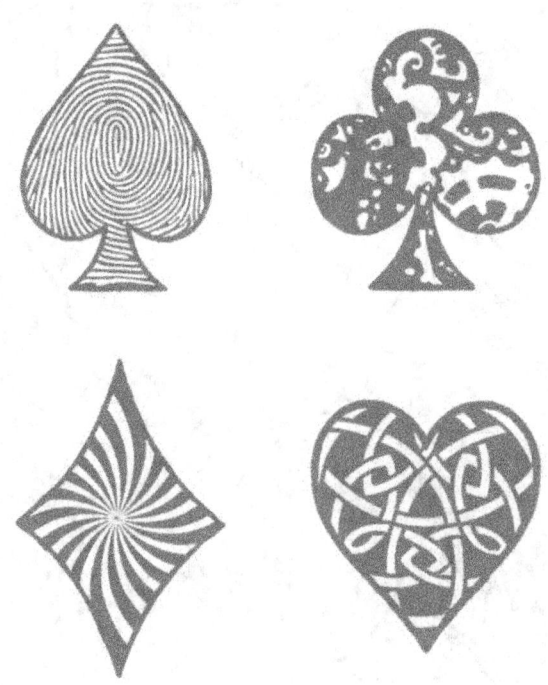

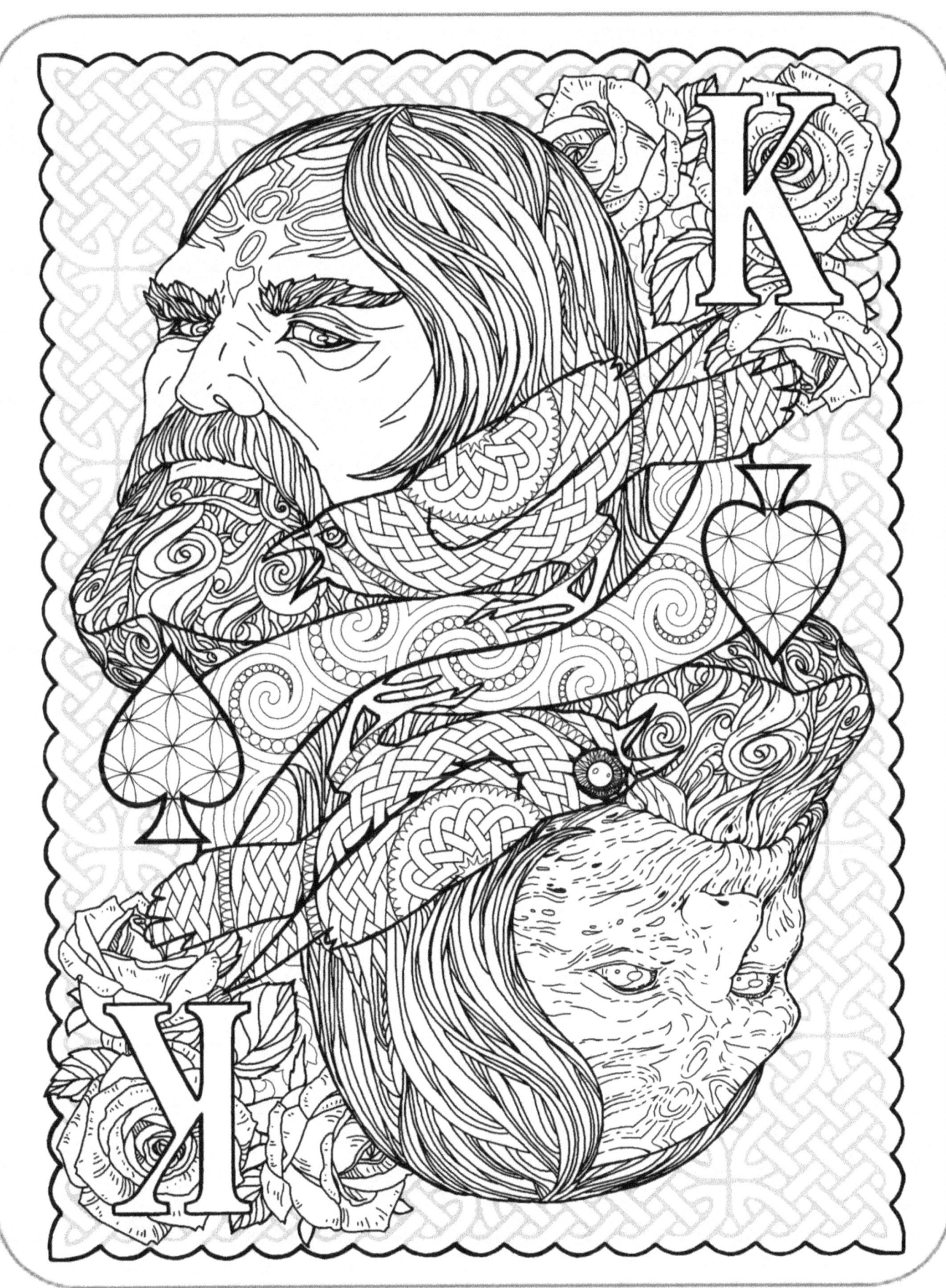

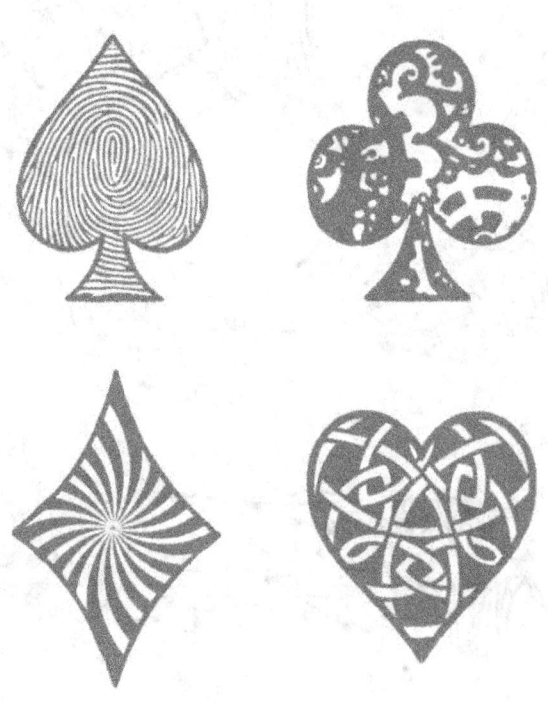

© Lisa Mitrokhin

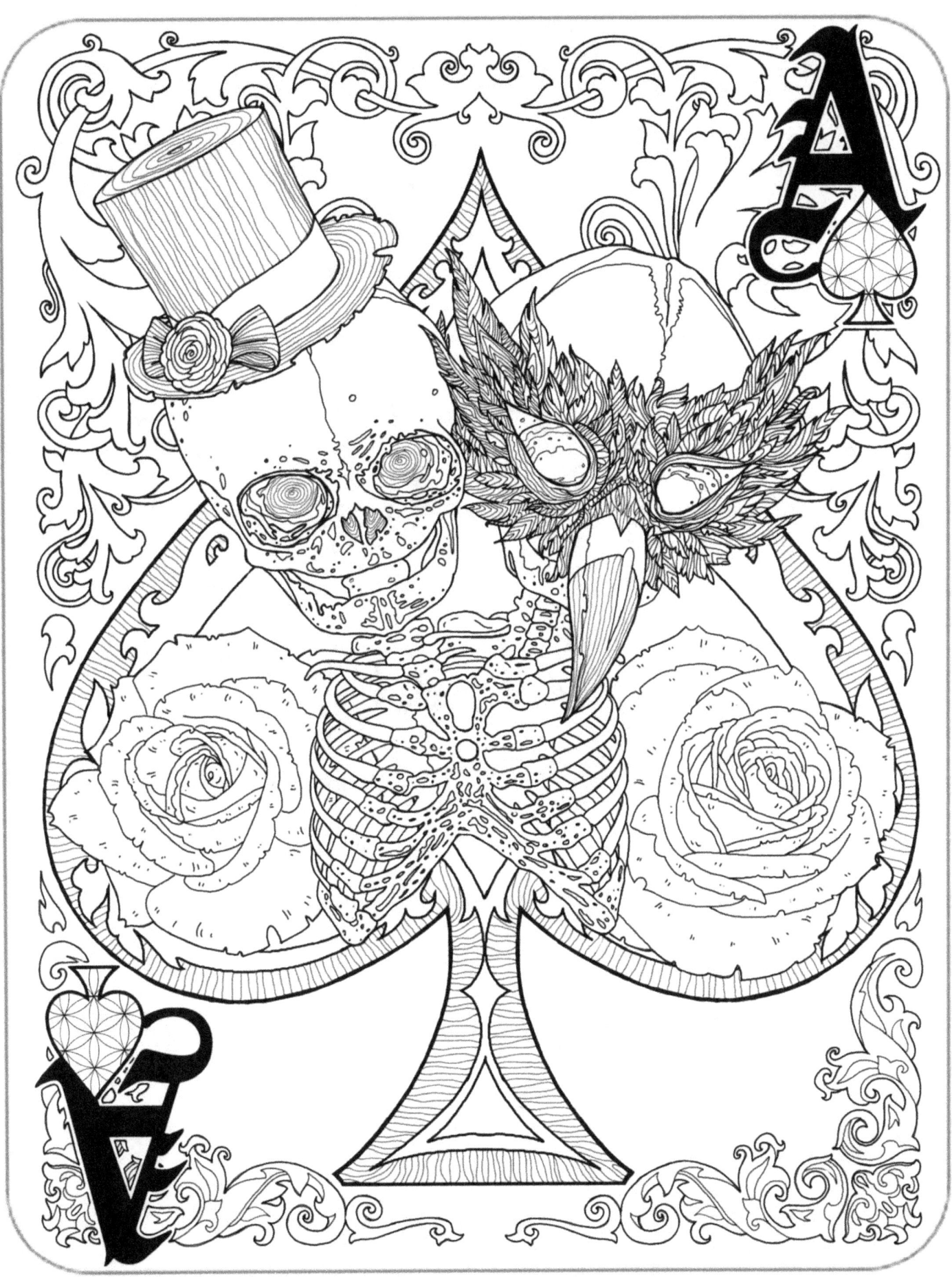

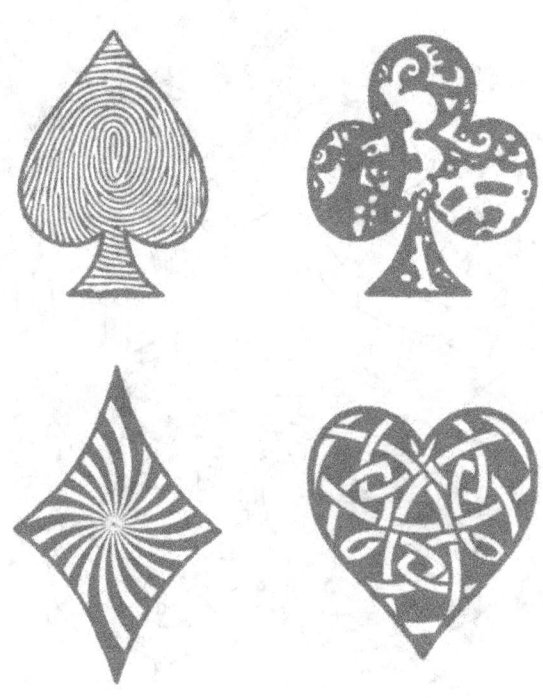

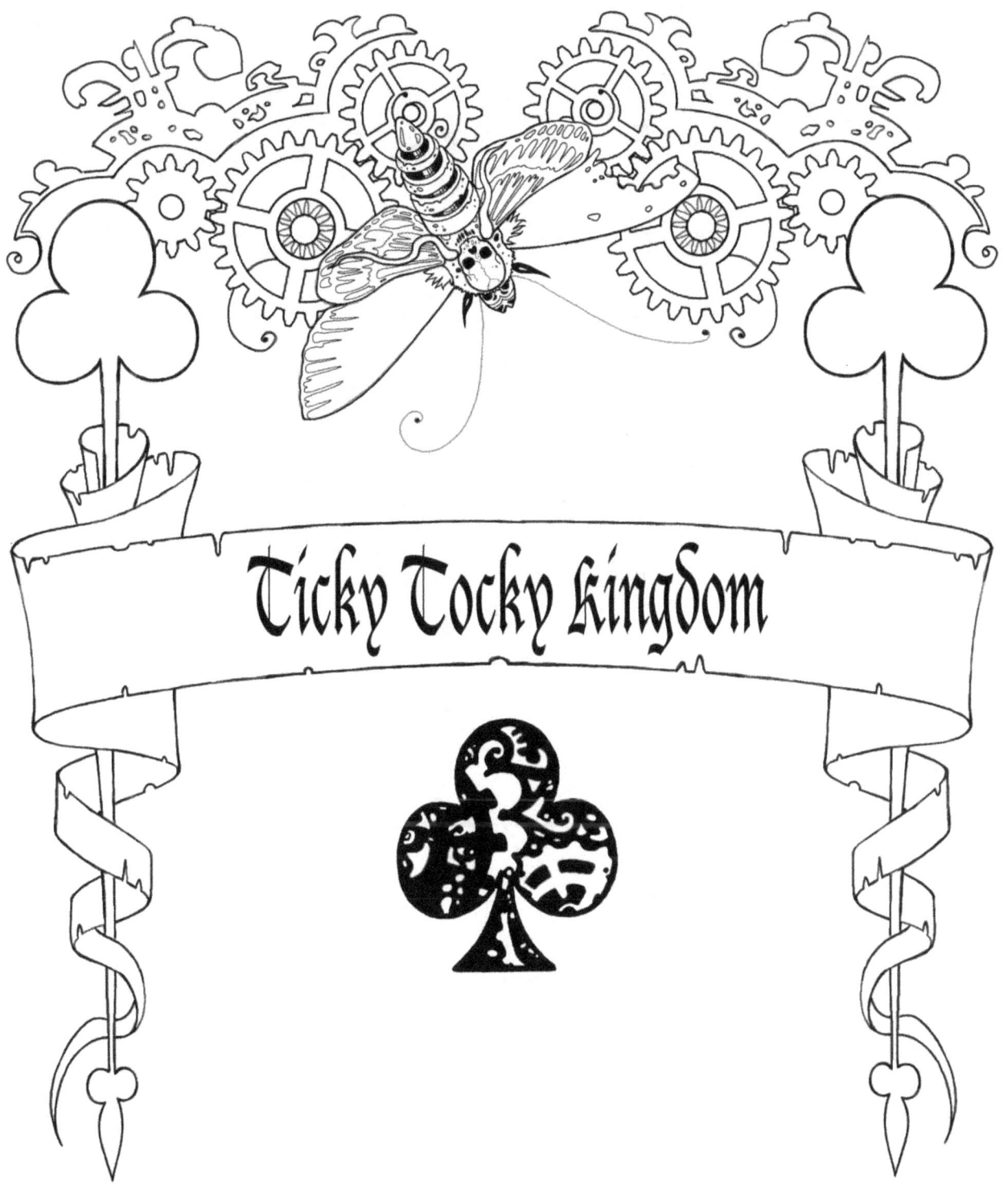

Ticky Tocky Kingdom

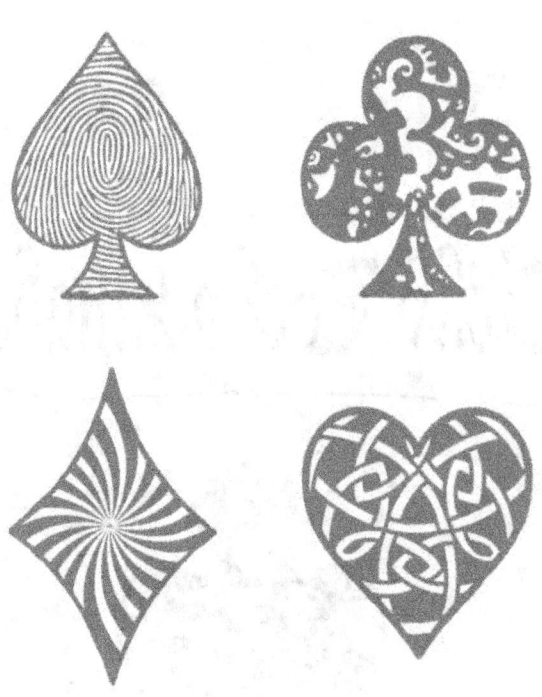

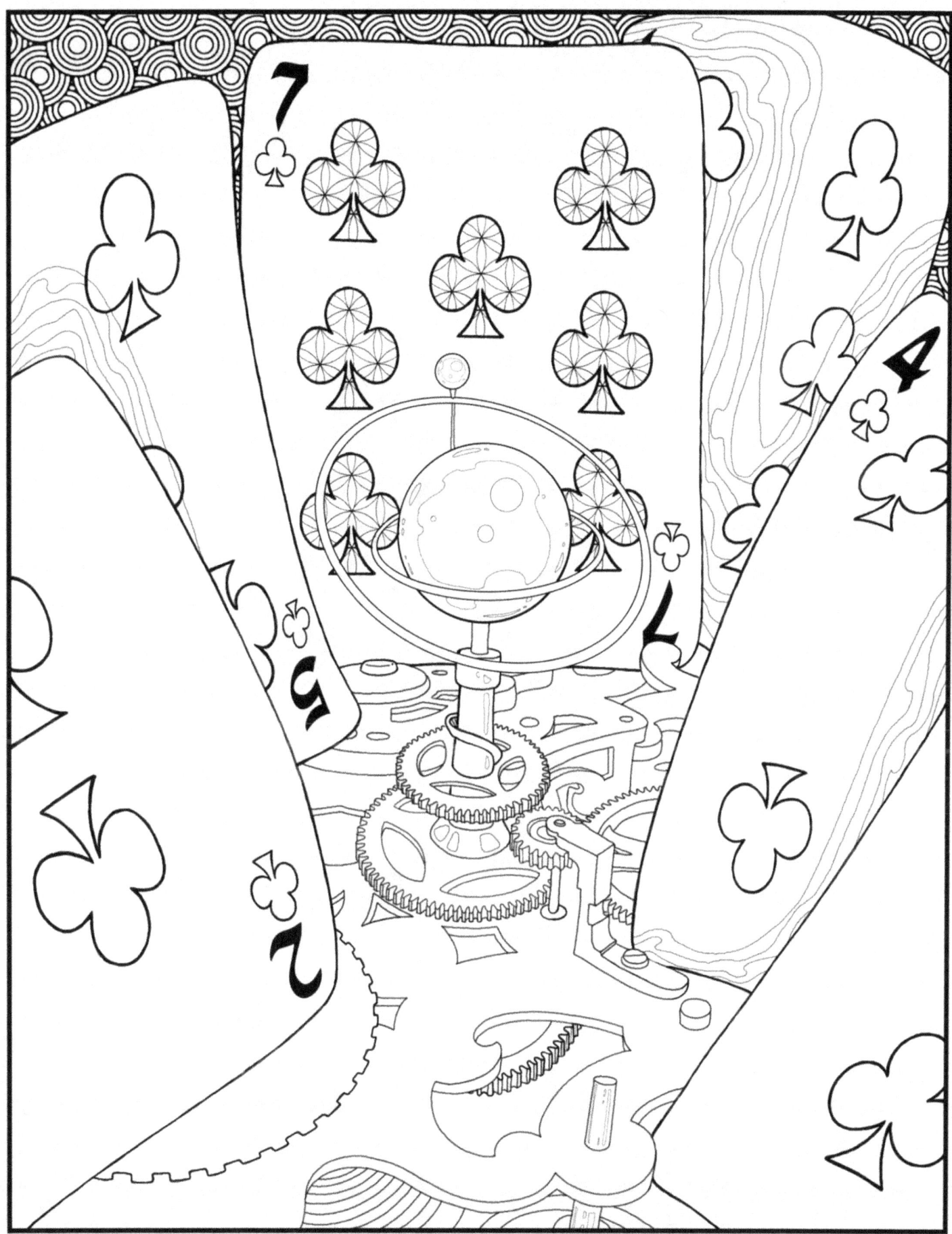

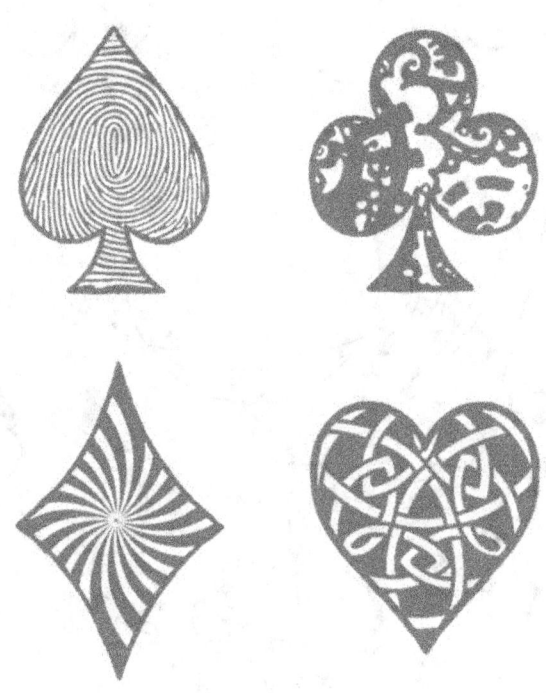

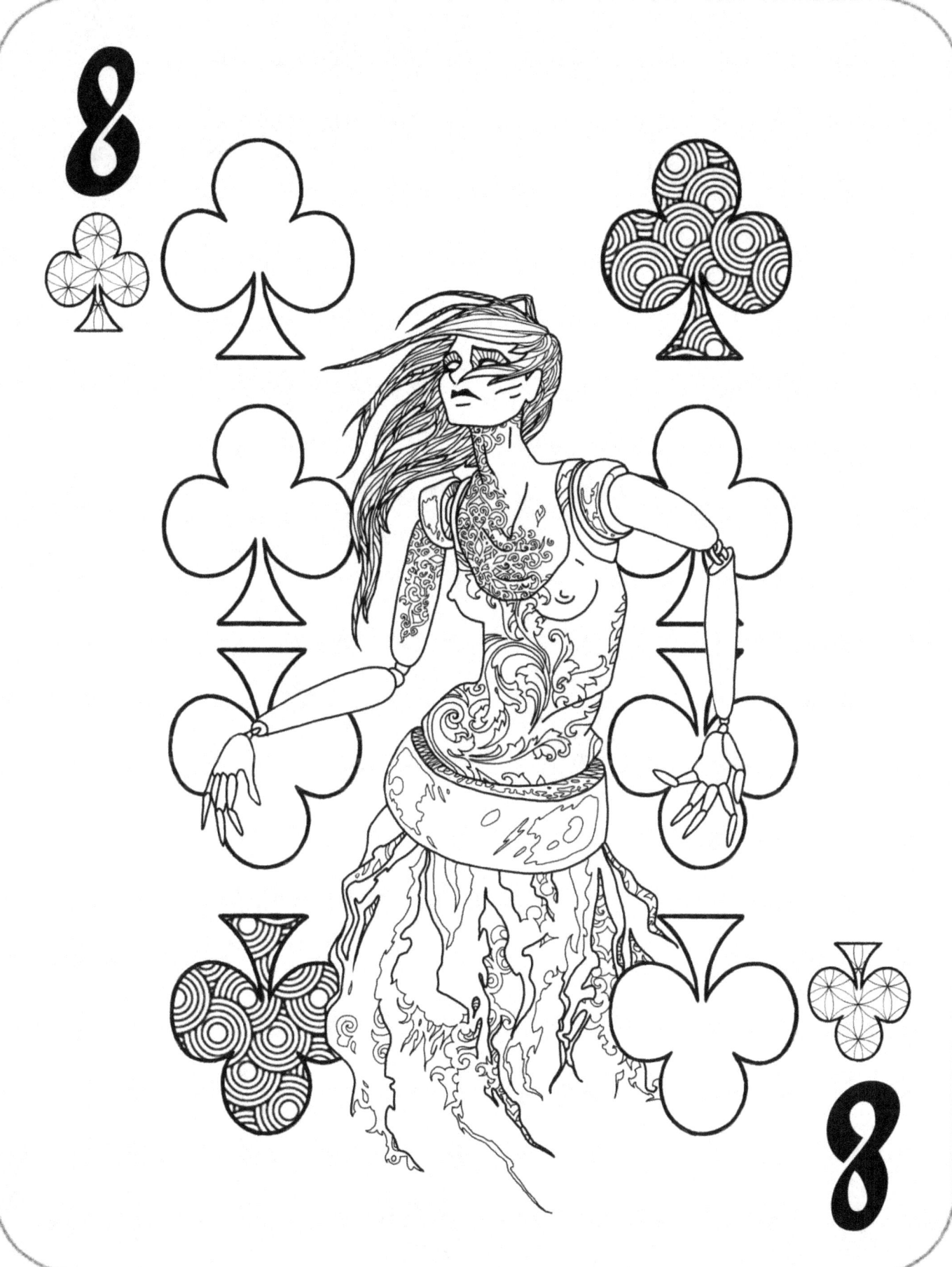

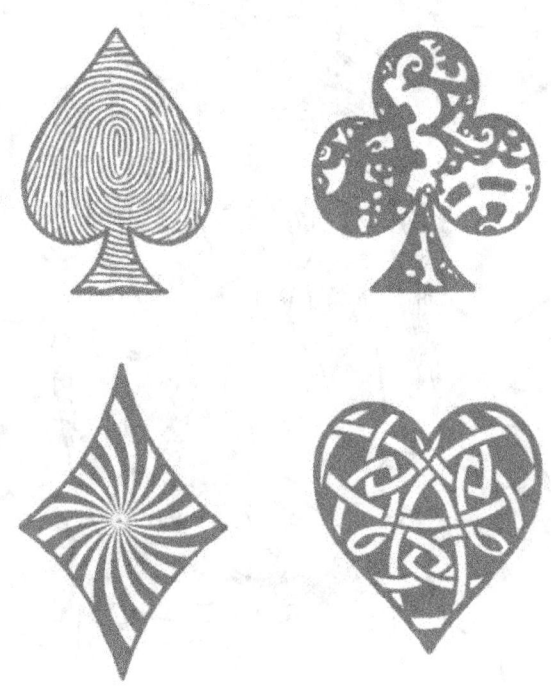

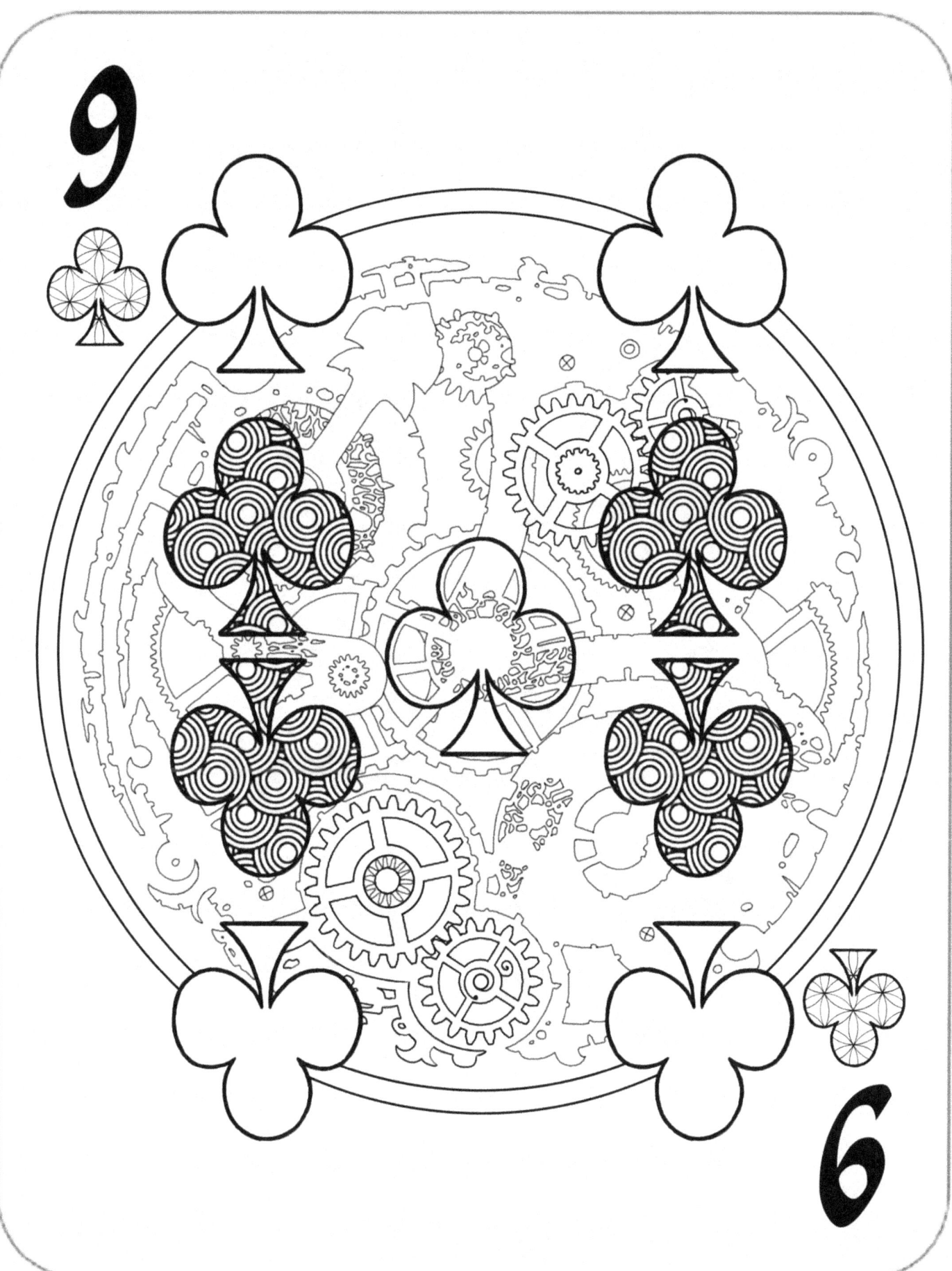

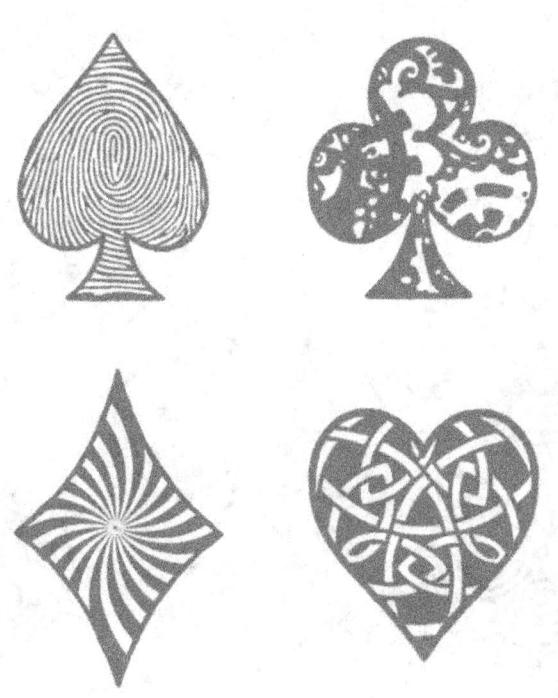

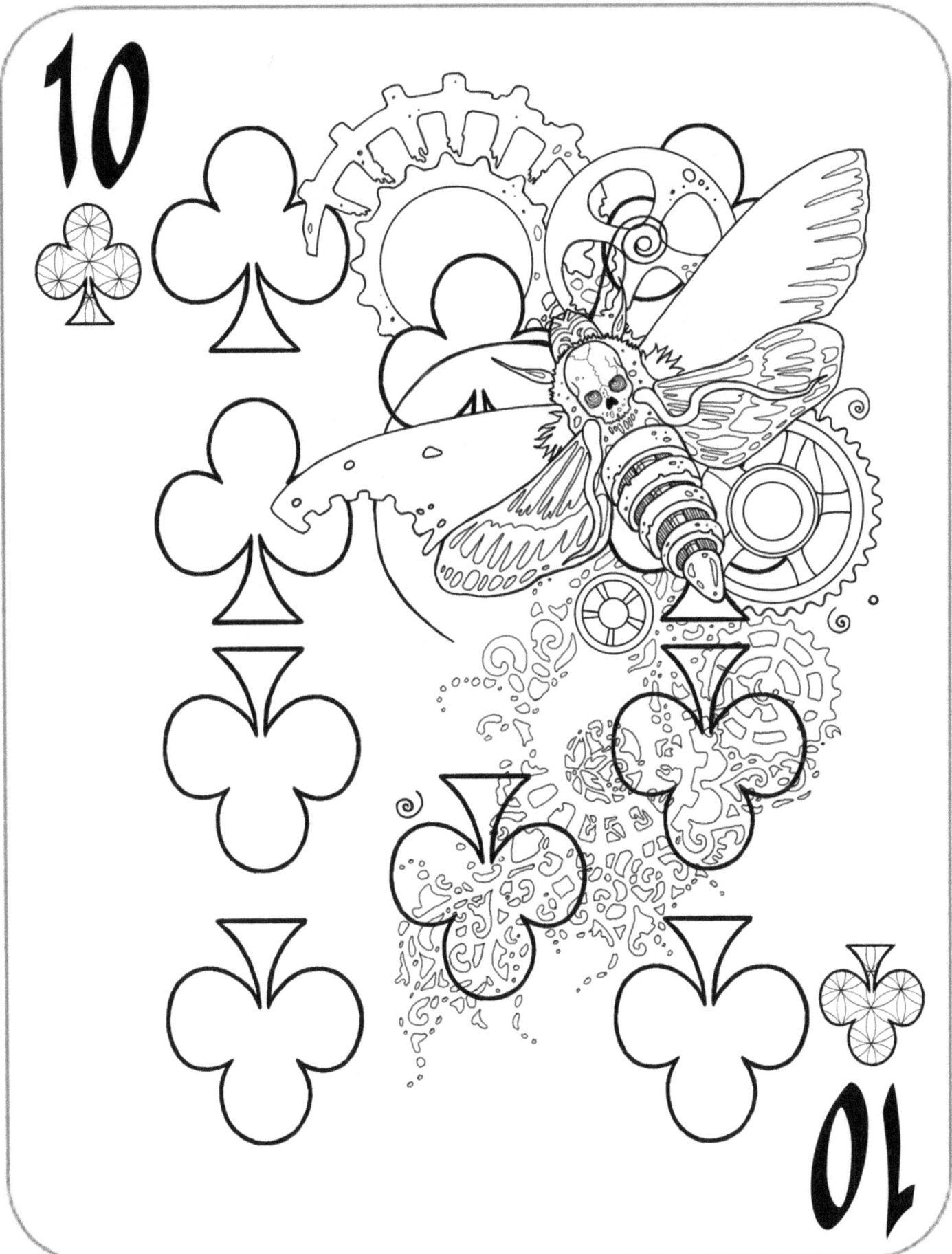

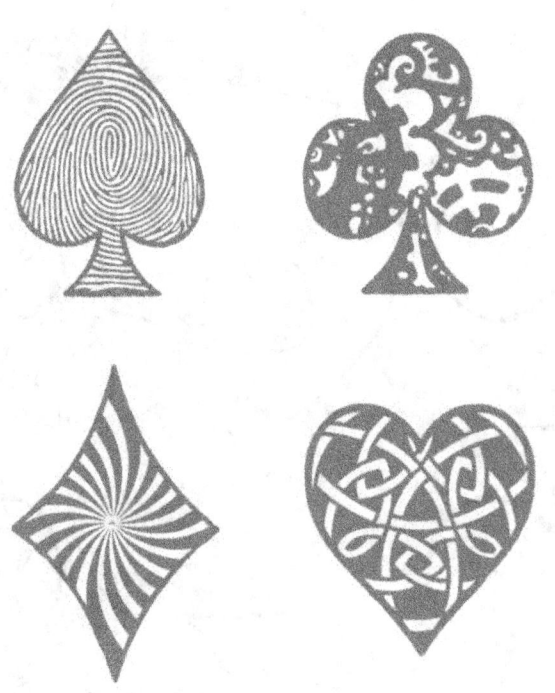

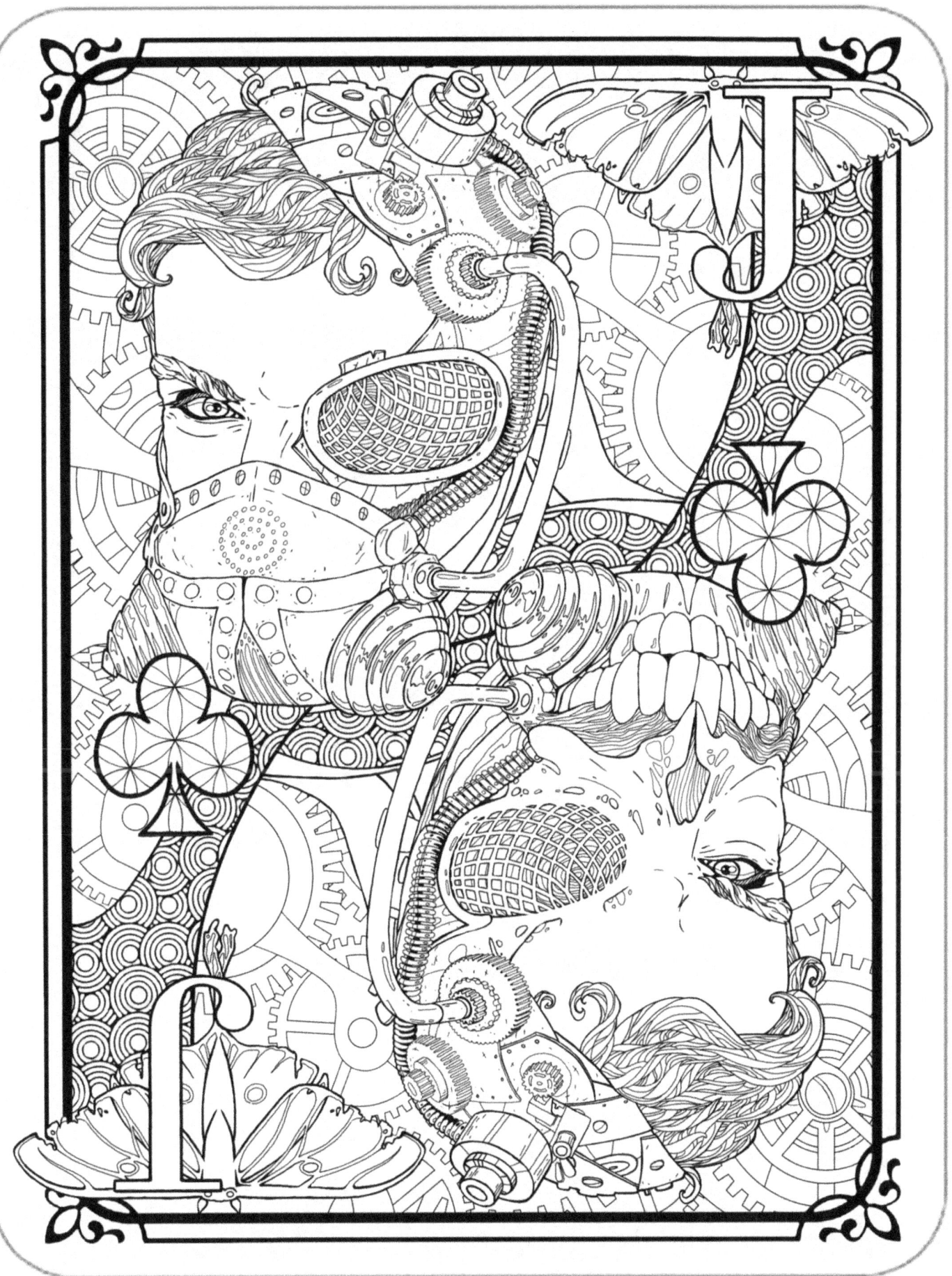

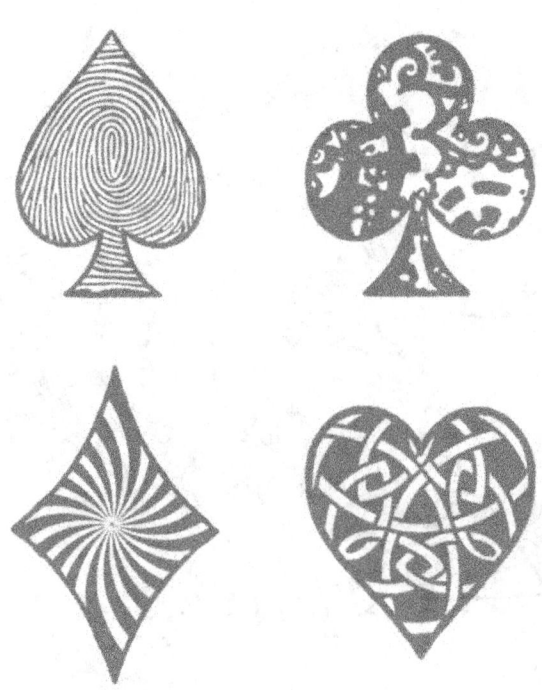

© Lisa Mitrokhin

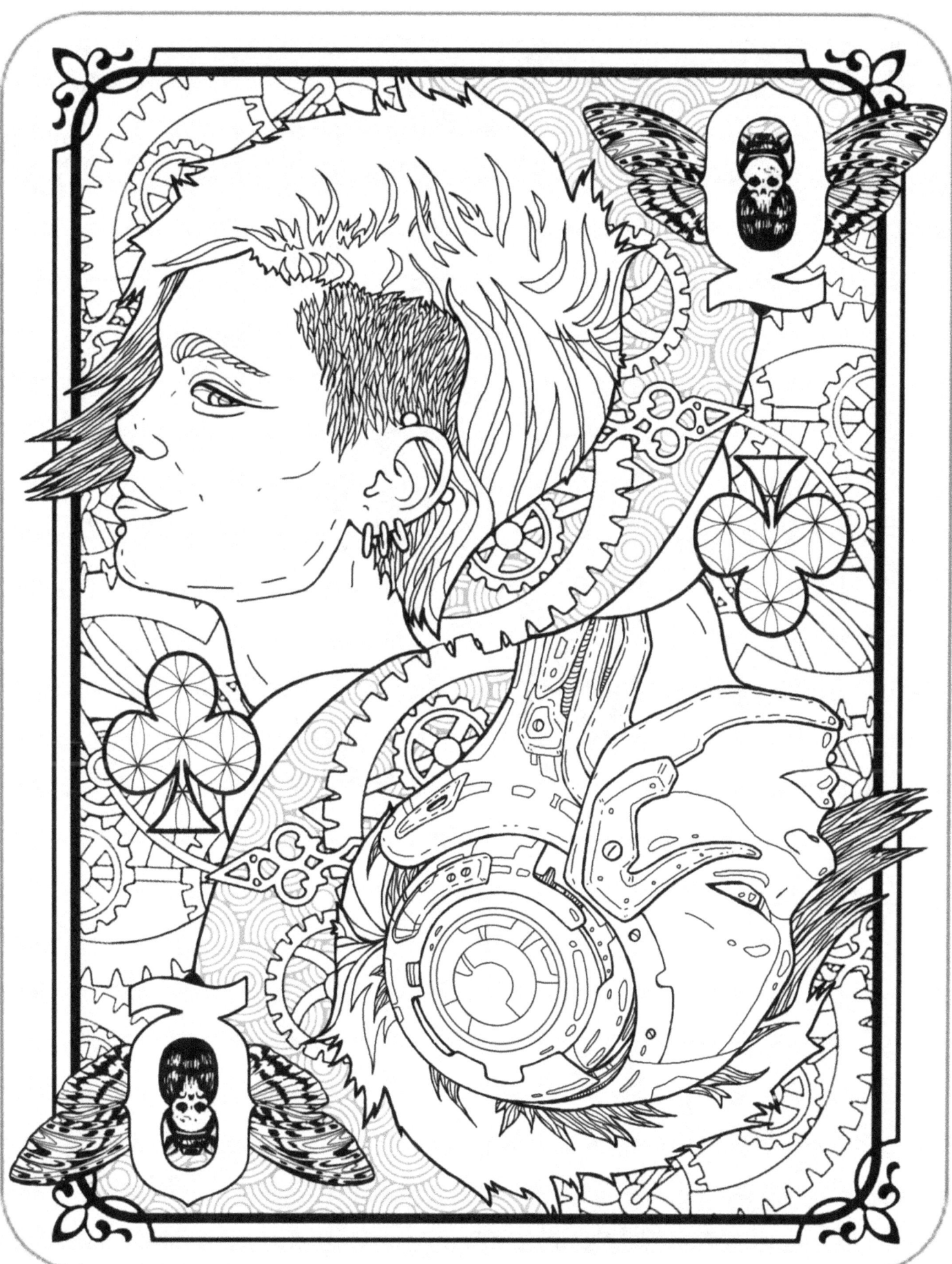

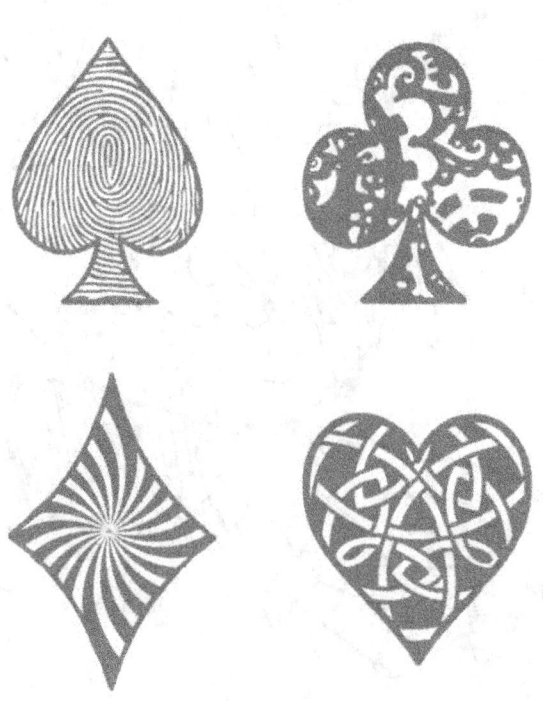

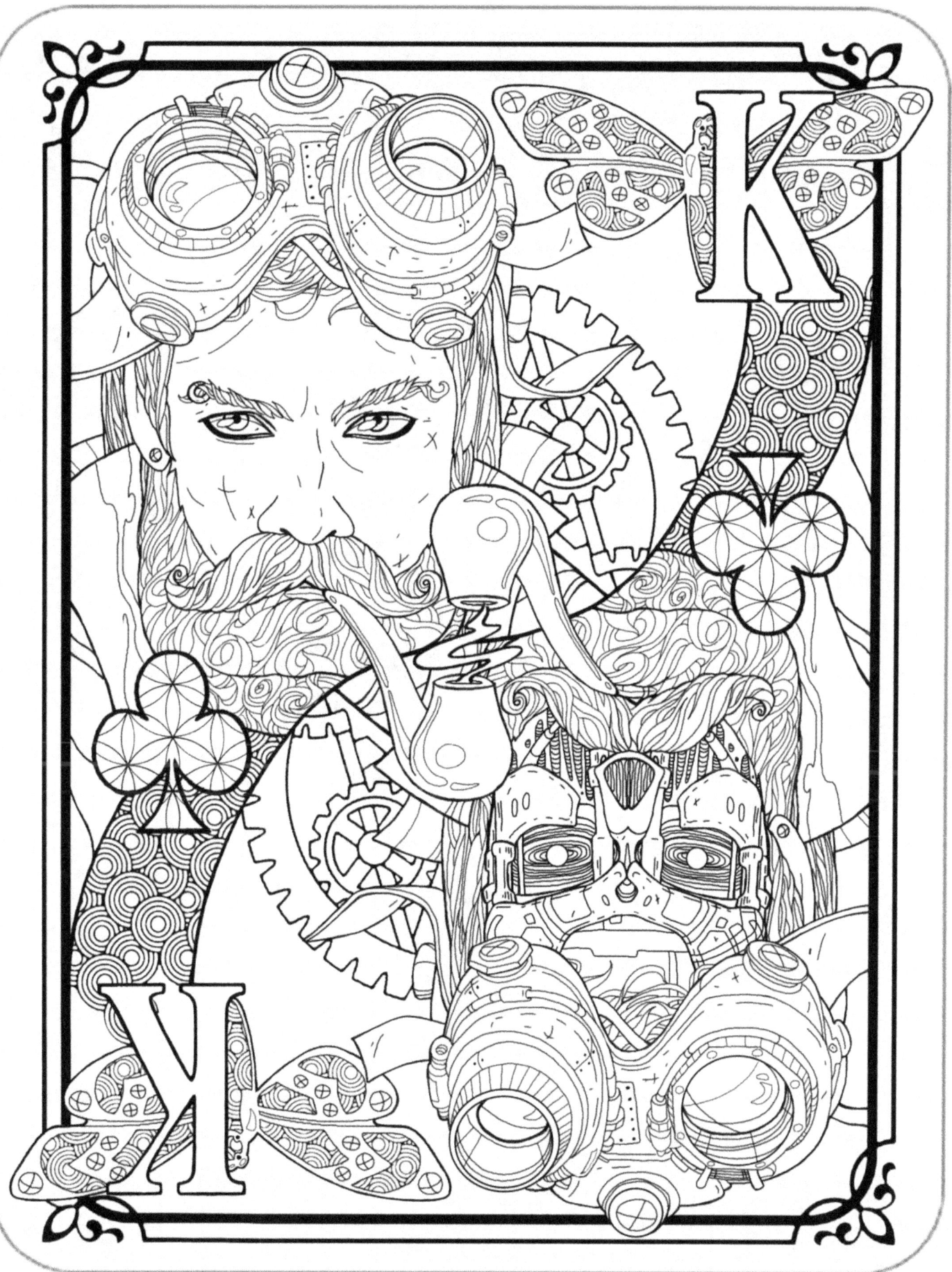

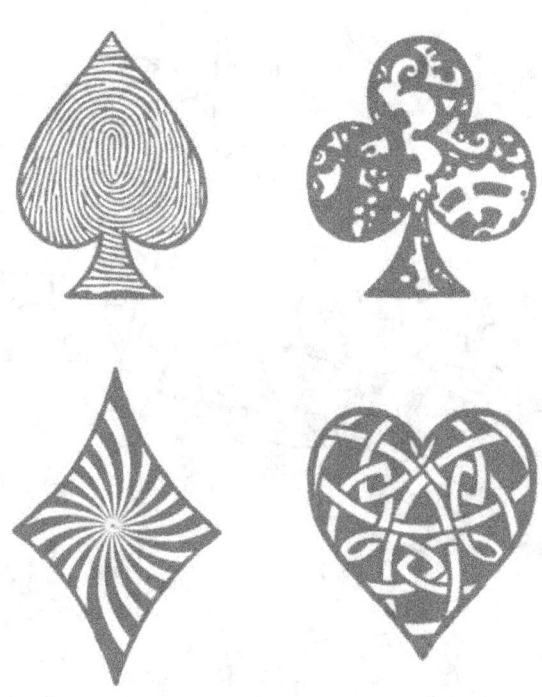

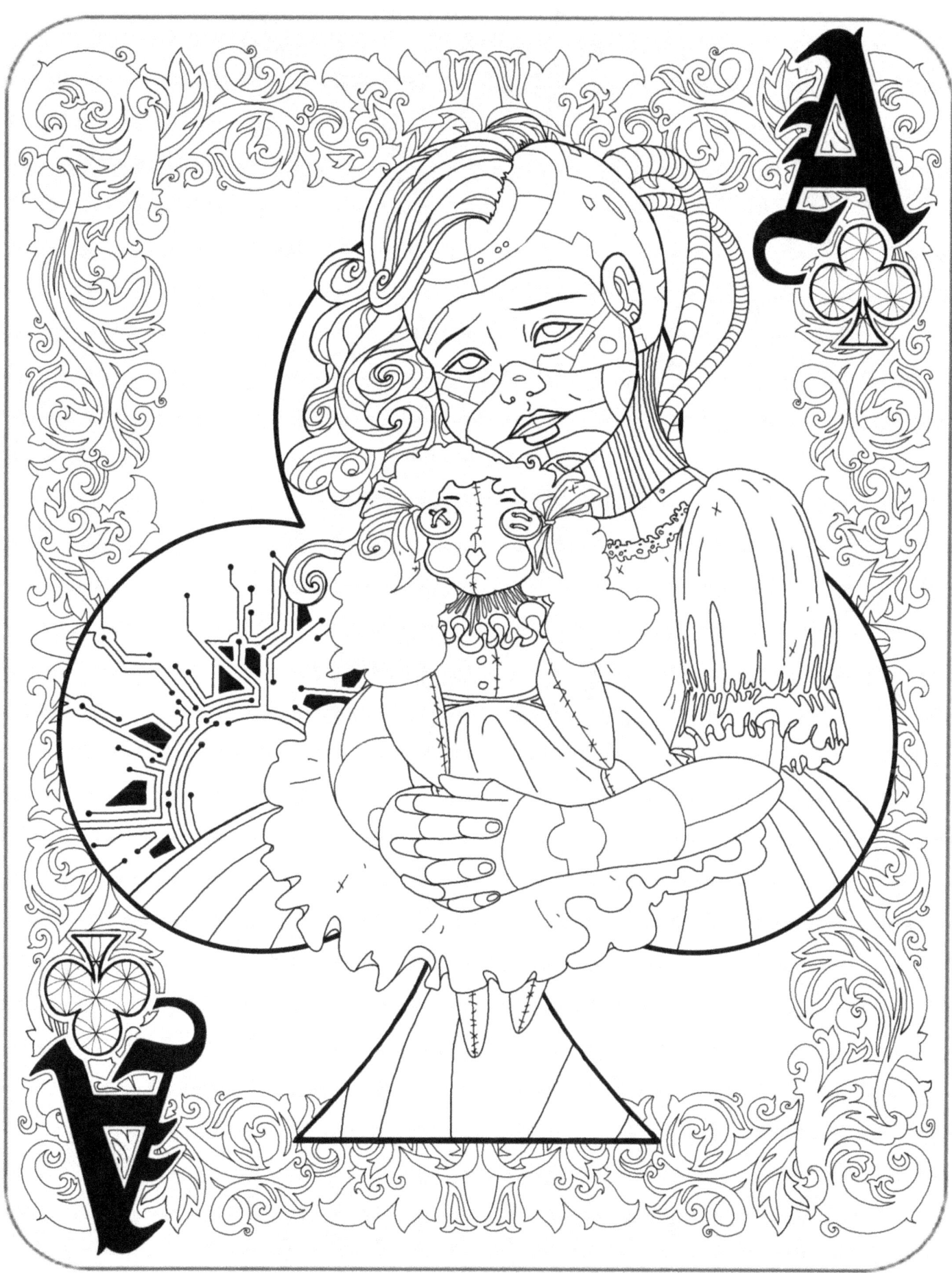

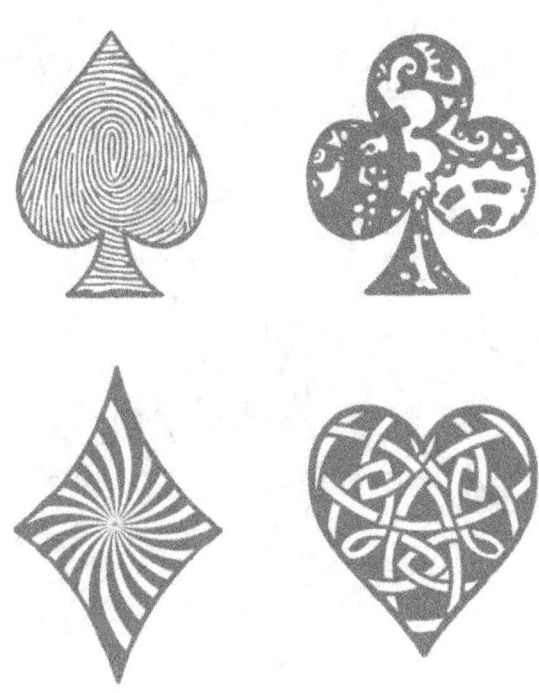

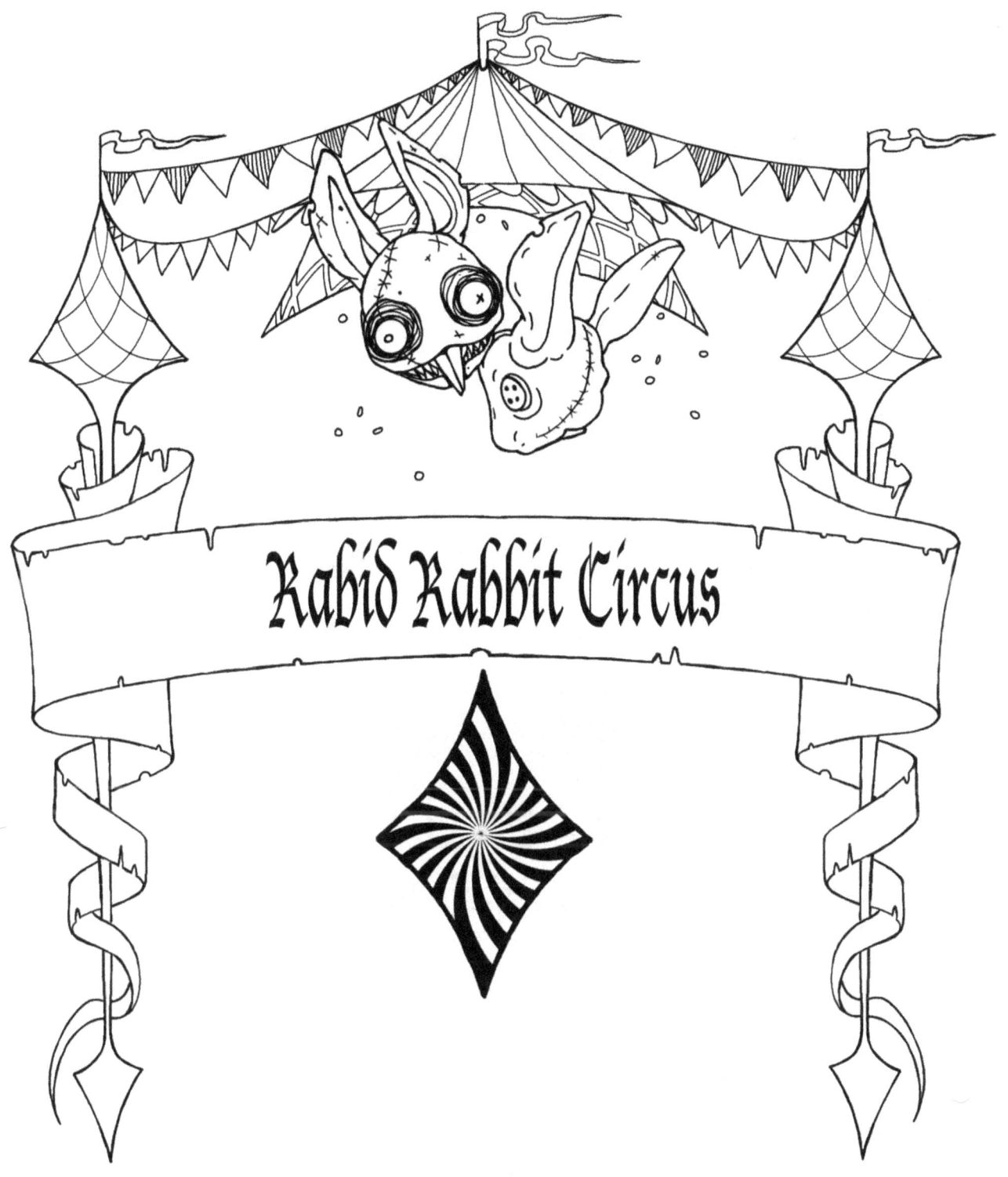

Rabid Rabbit Circus

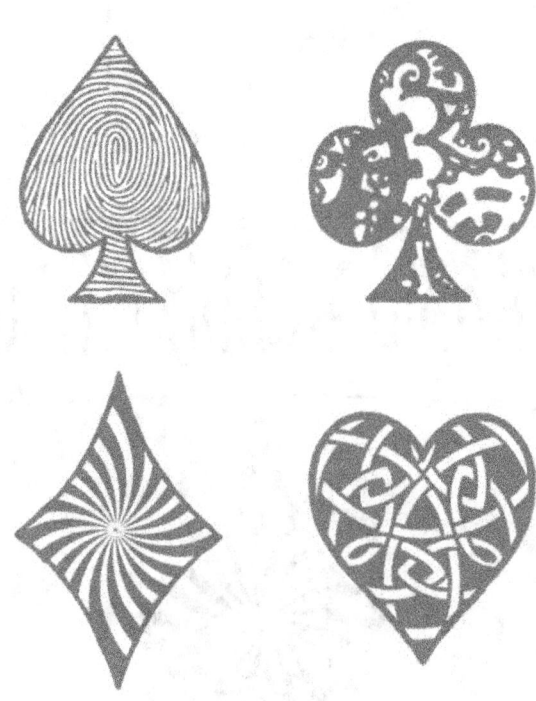

© Lisa Mitrokhin

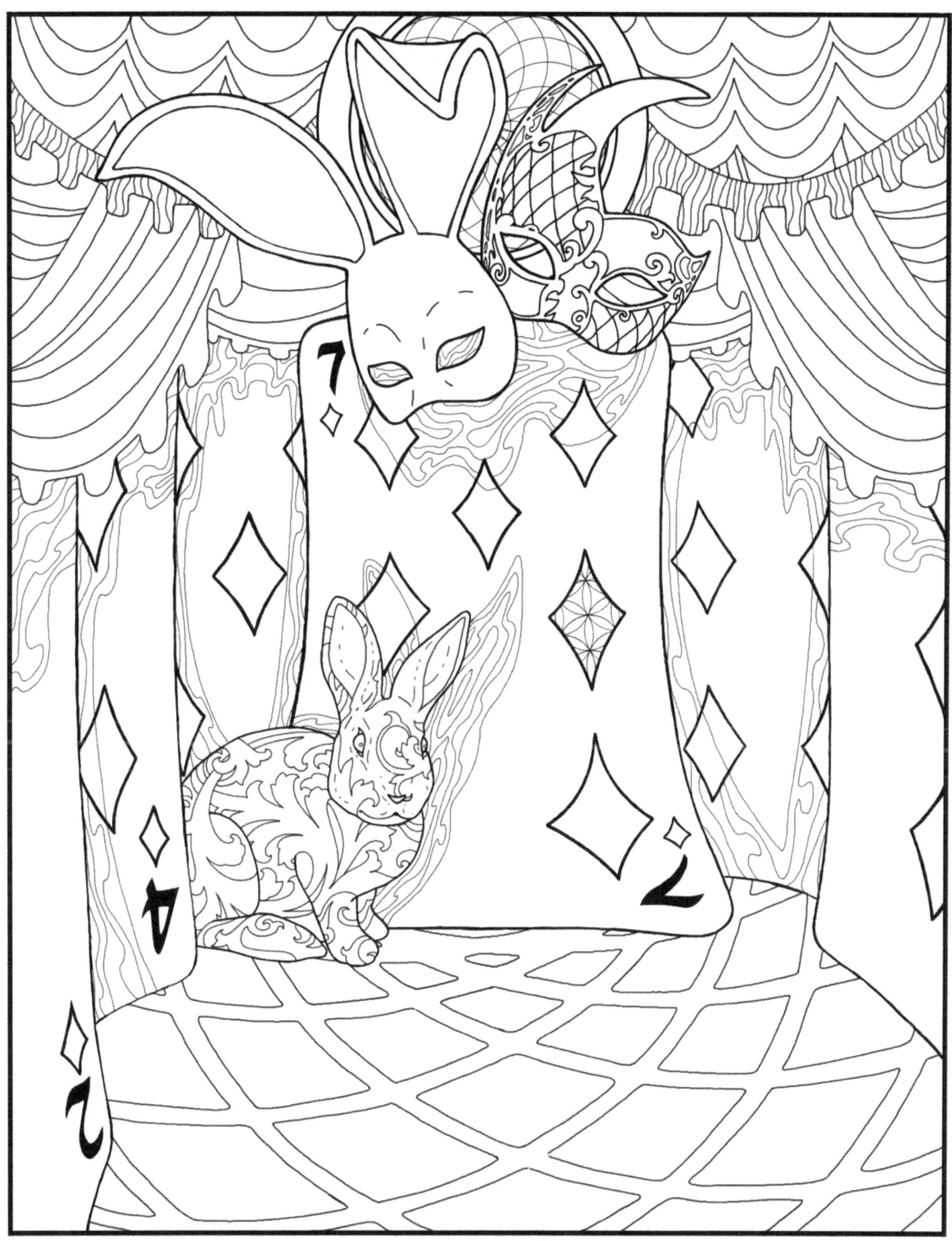

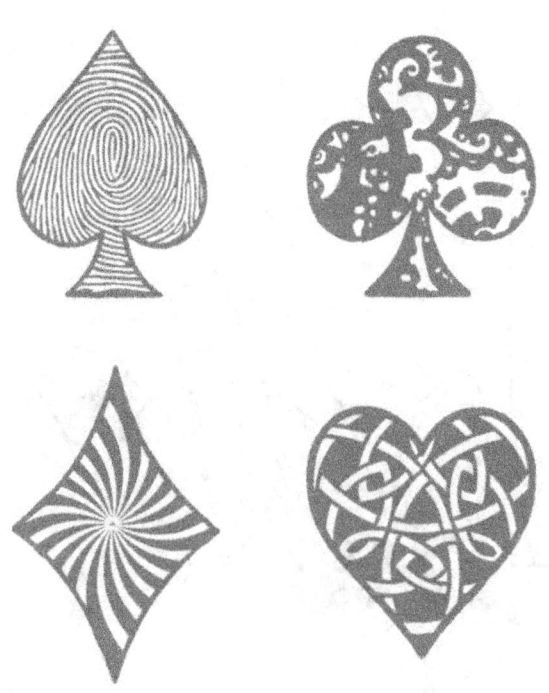

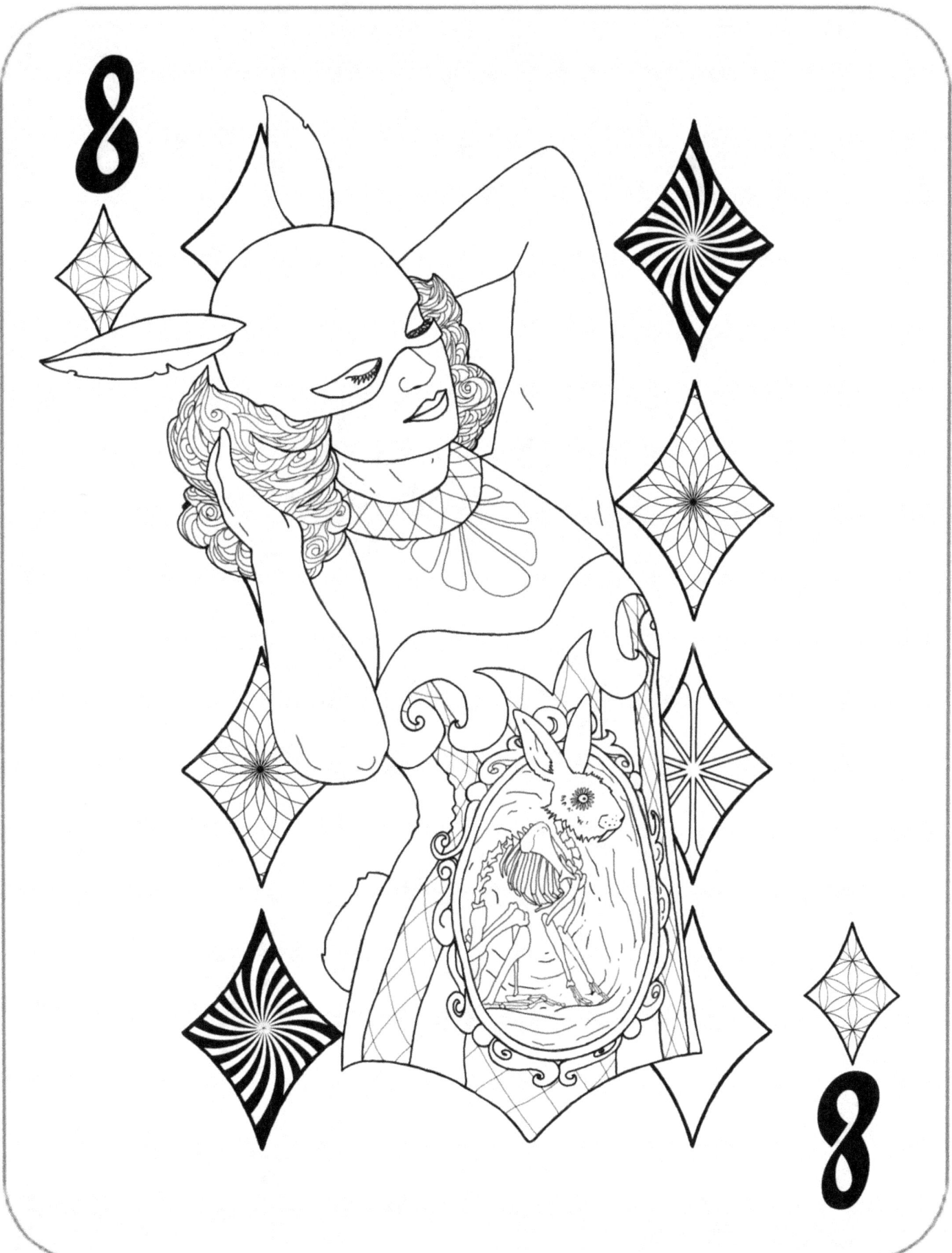

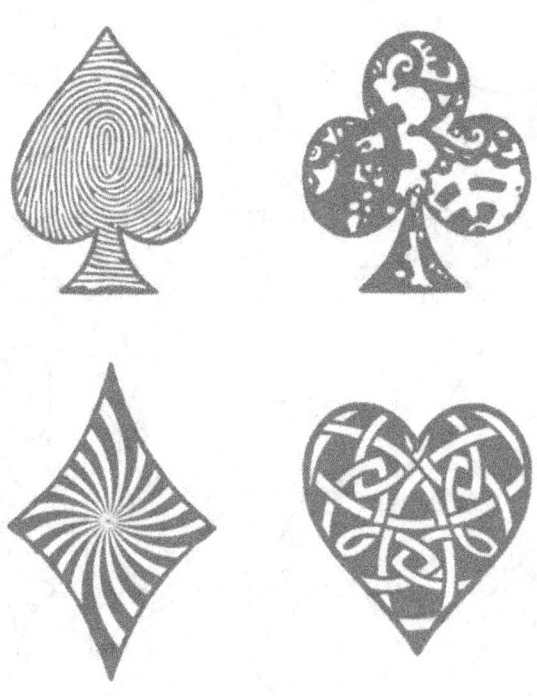

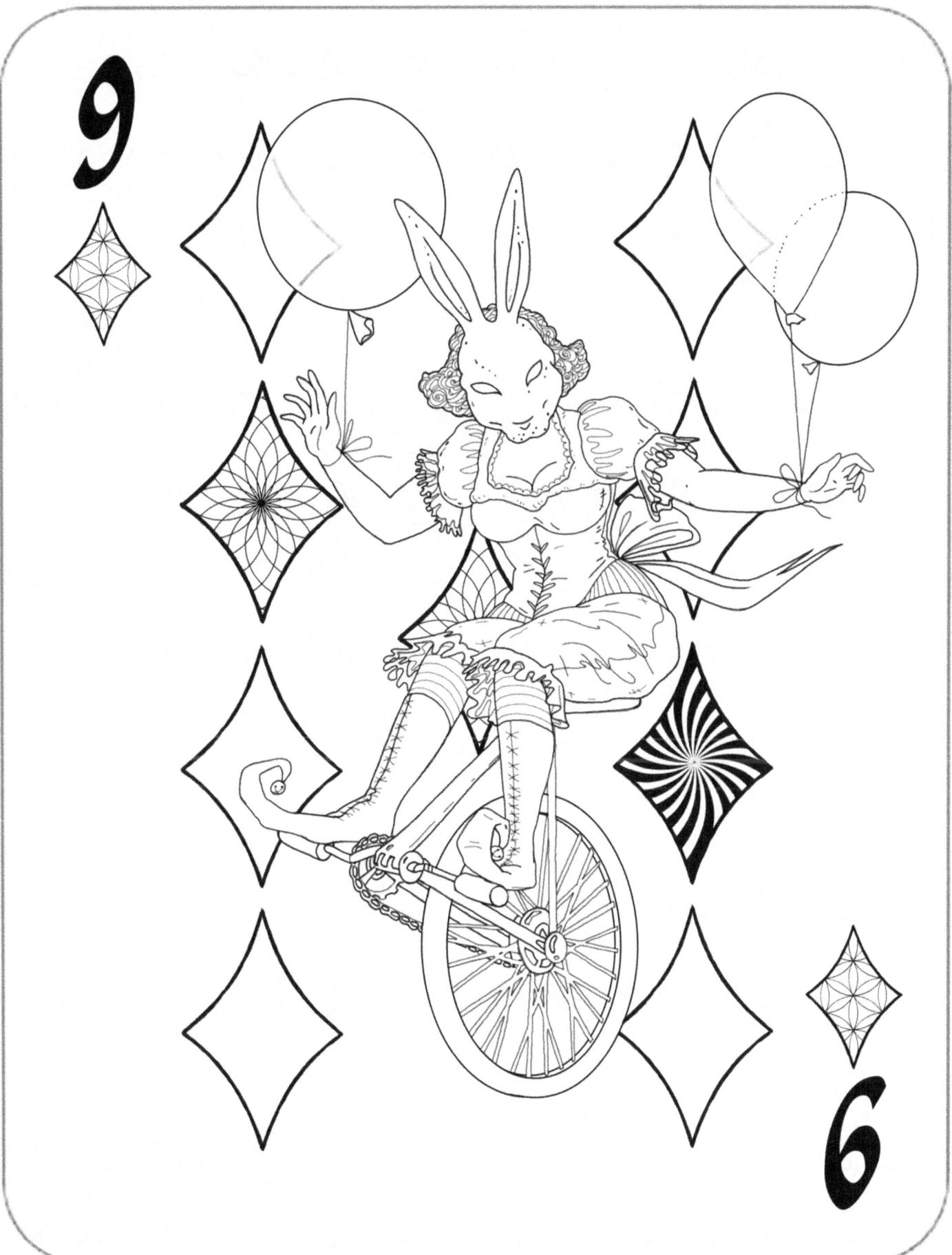

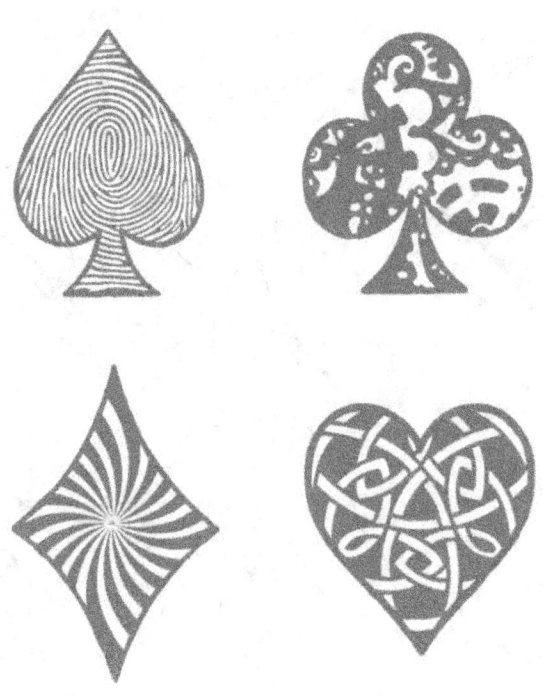

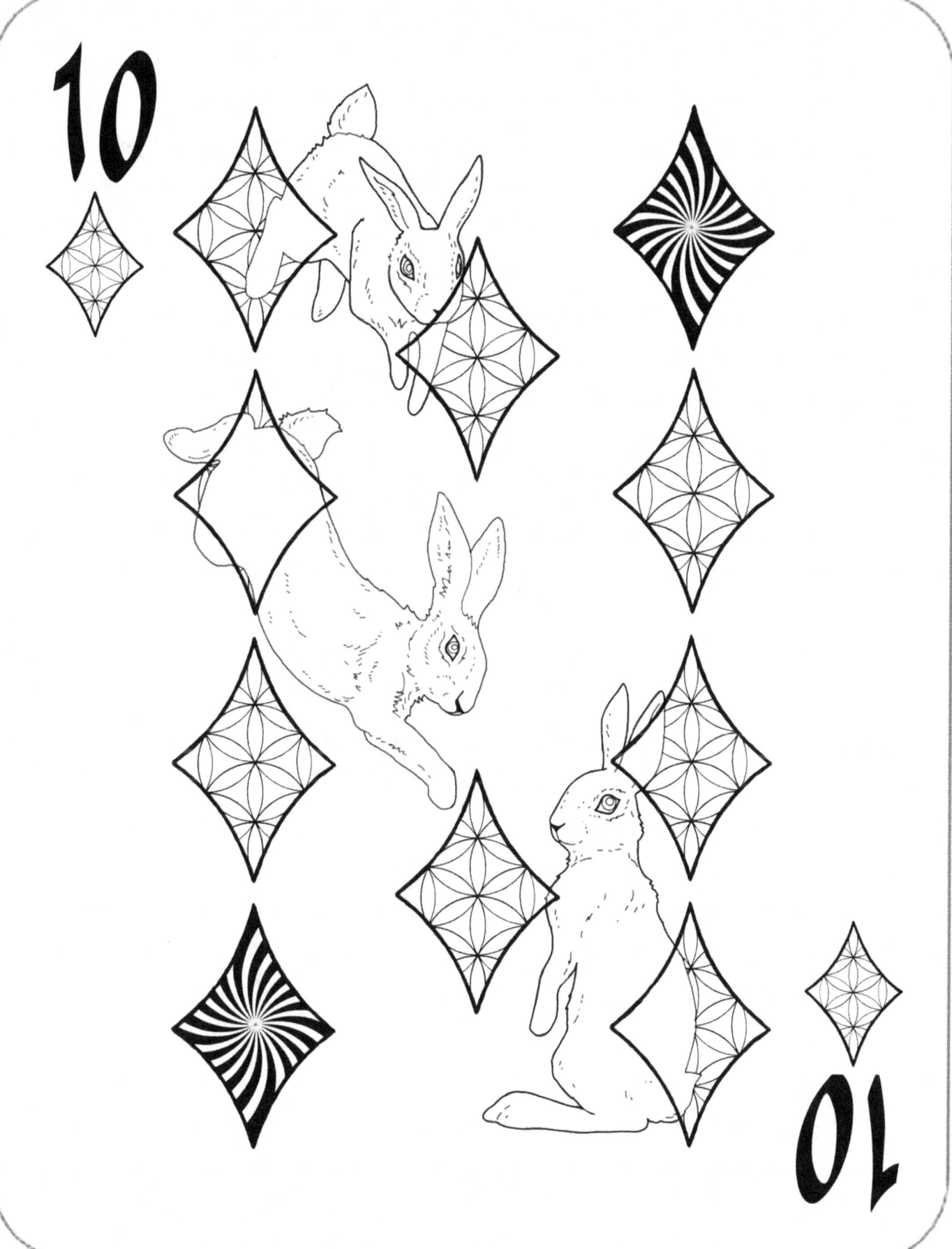

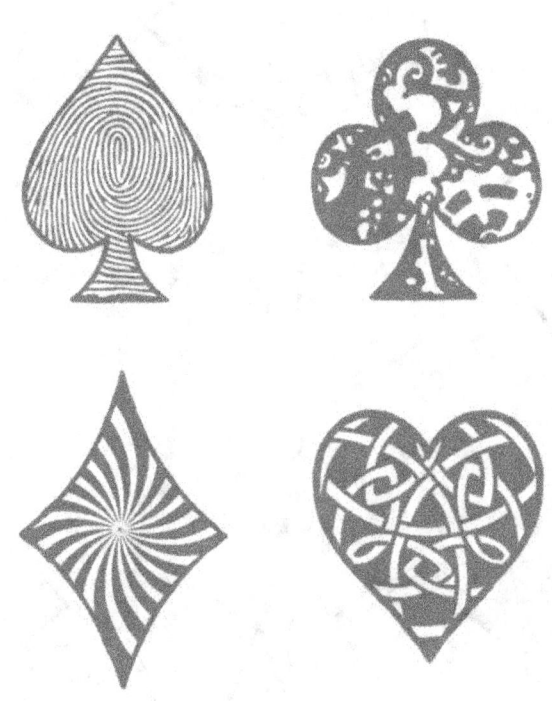

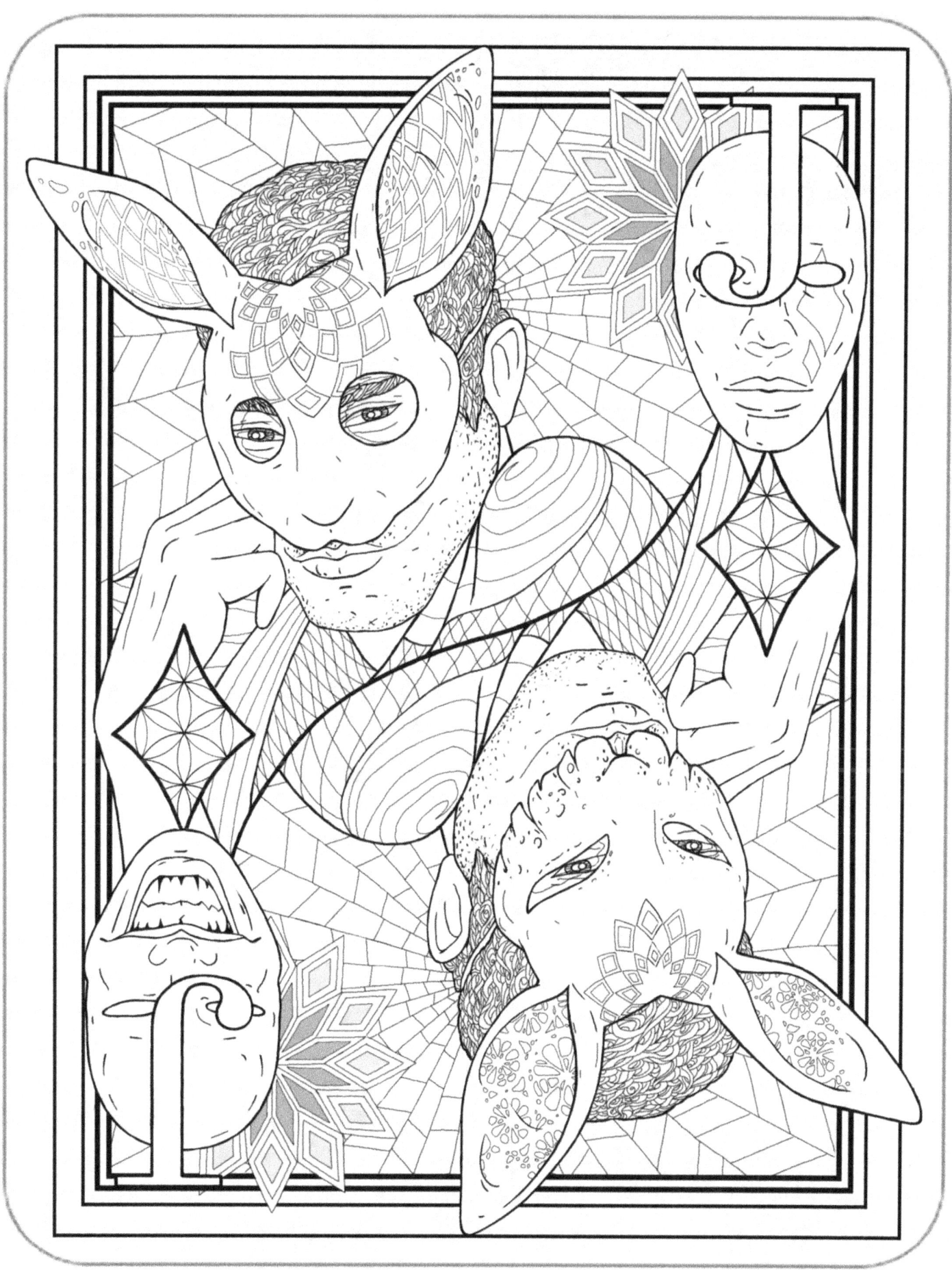

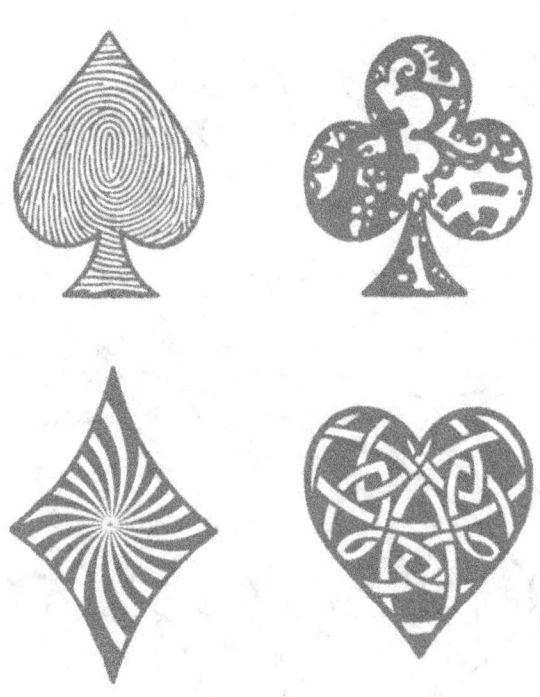

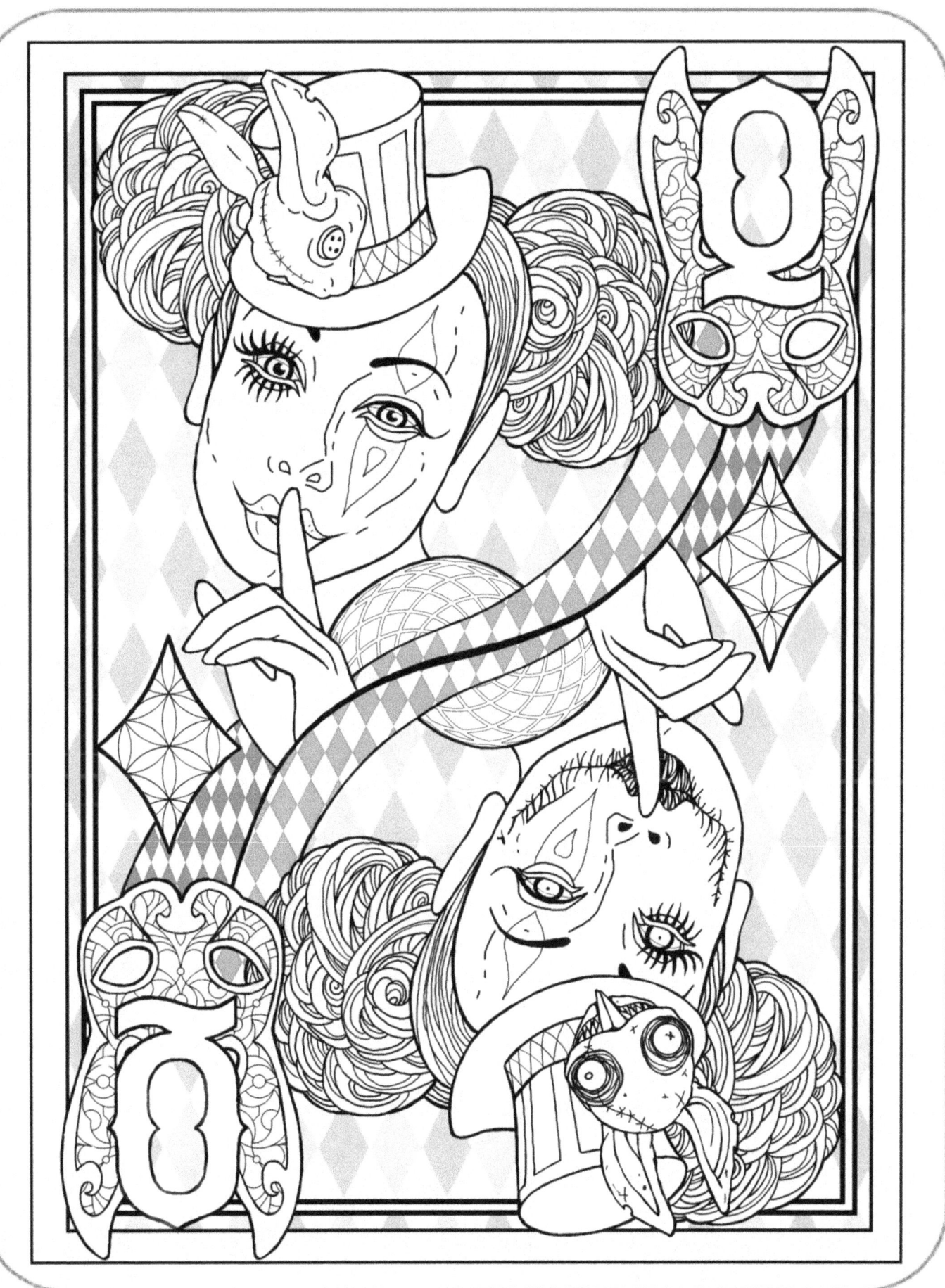

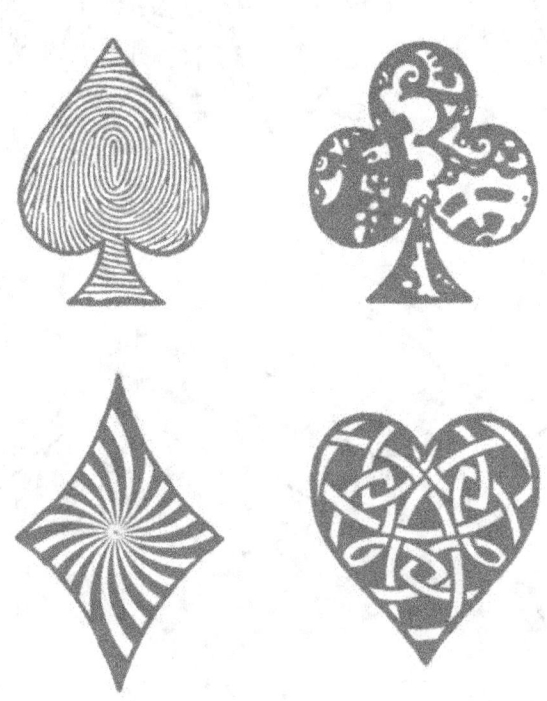

© Lisa Mitrokhin

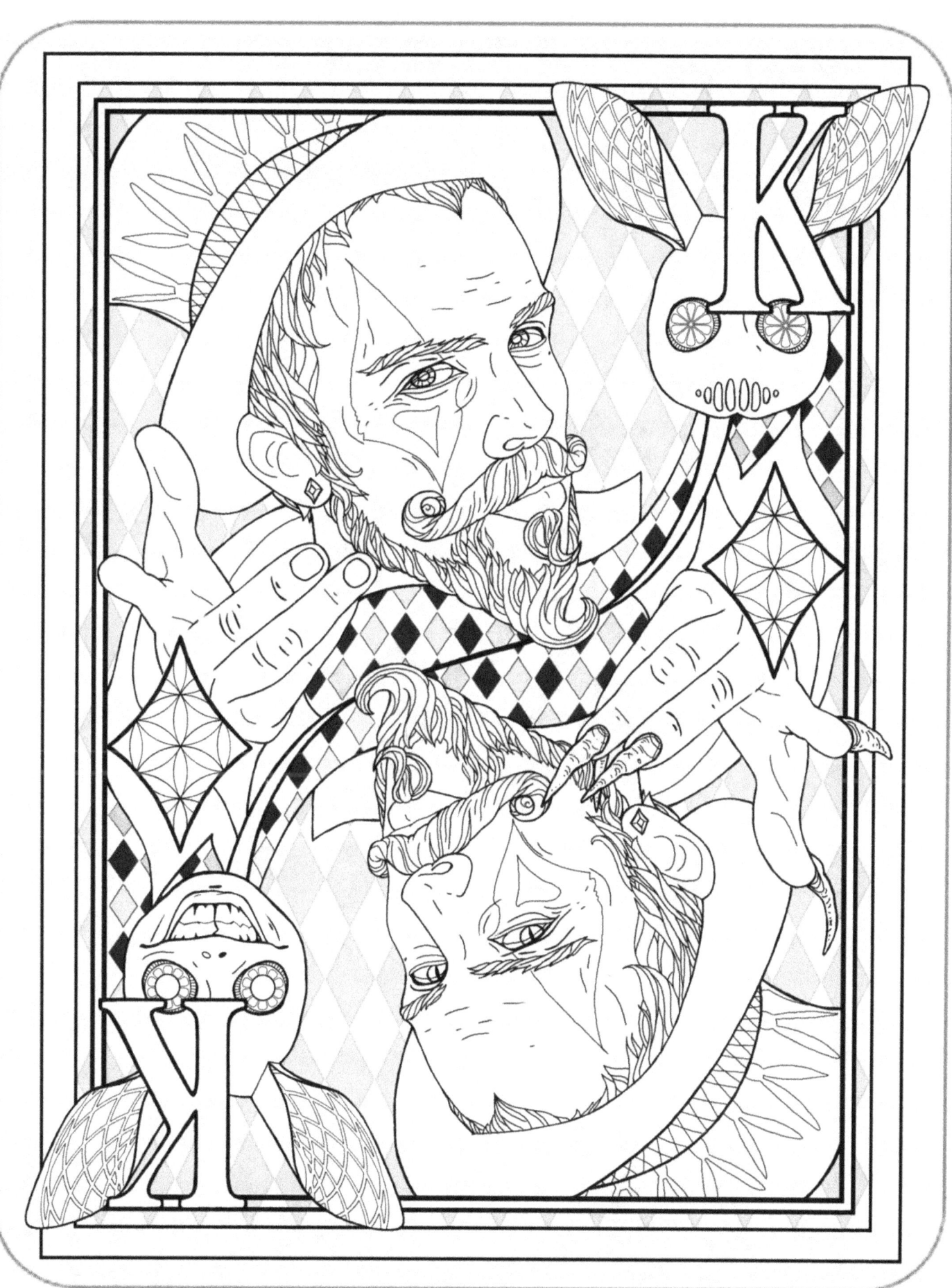

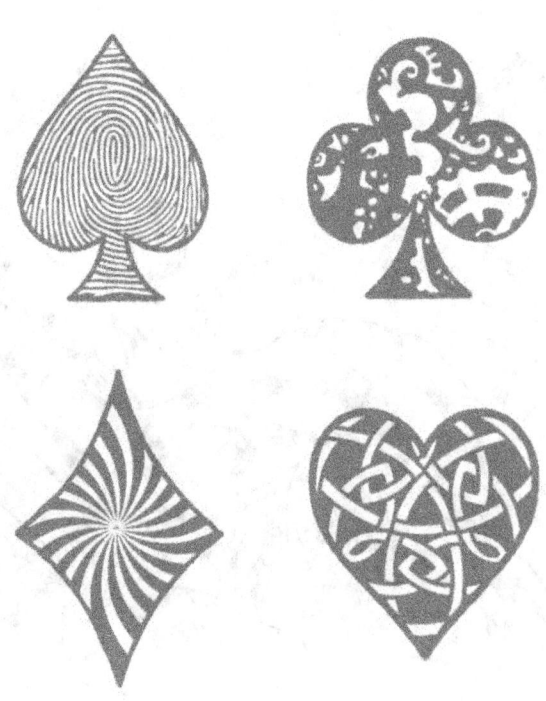

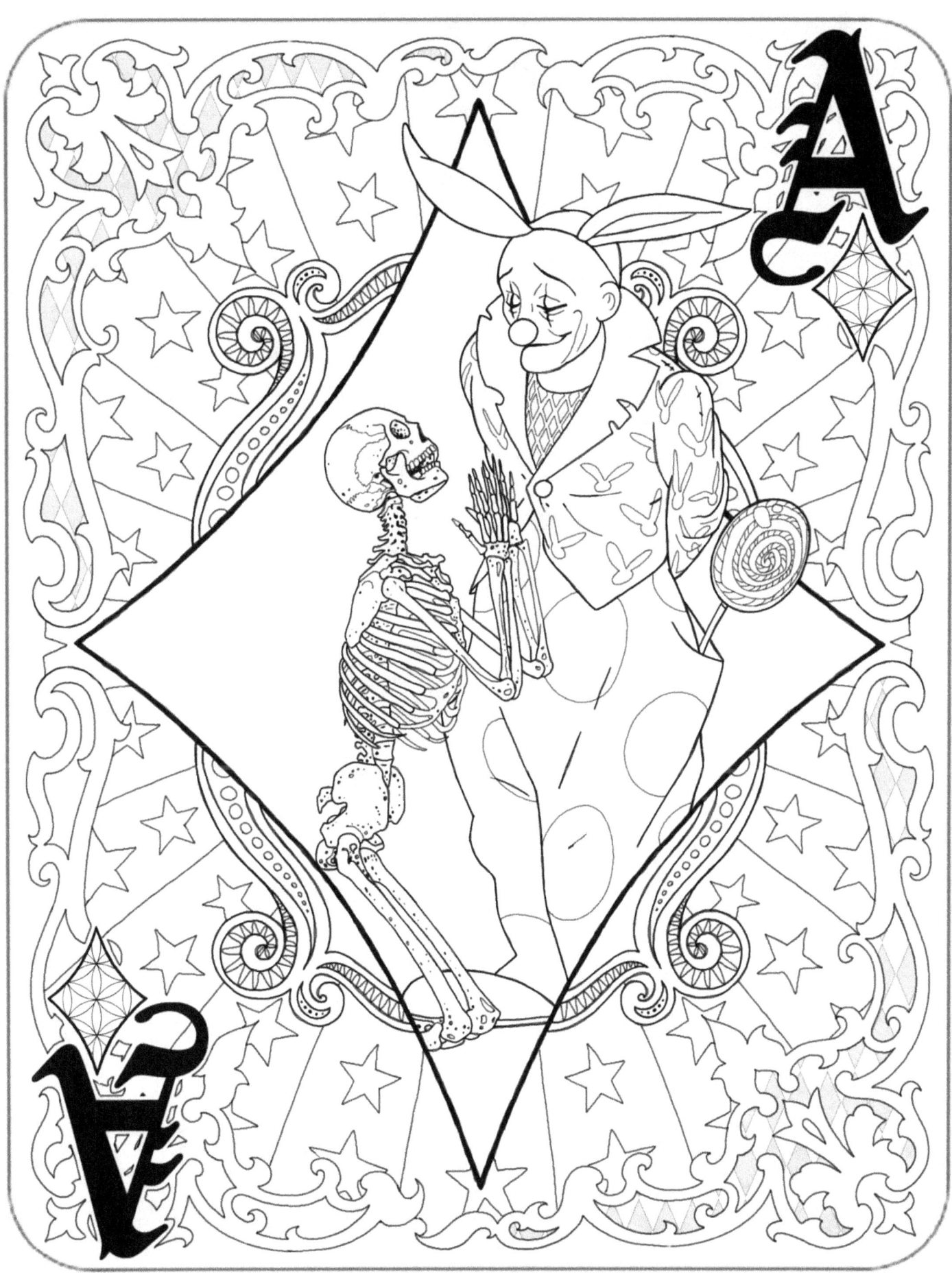

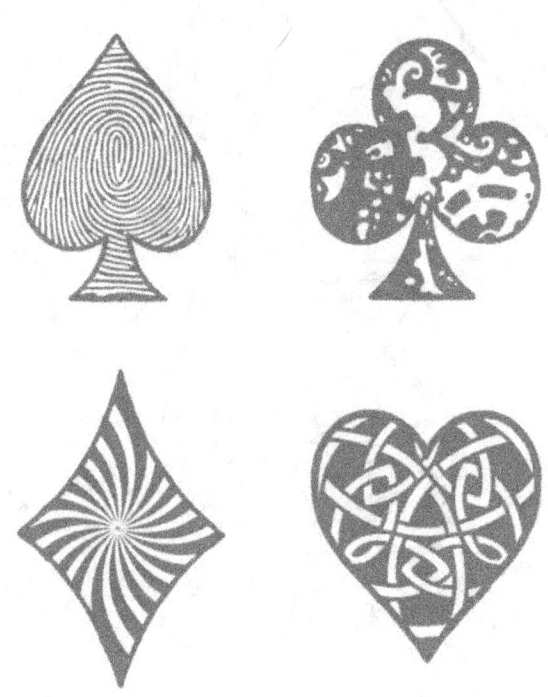

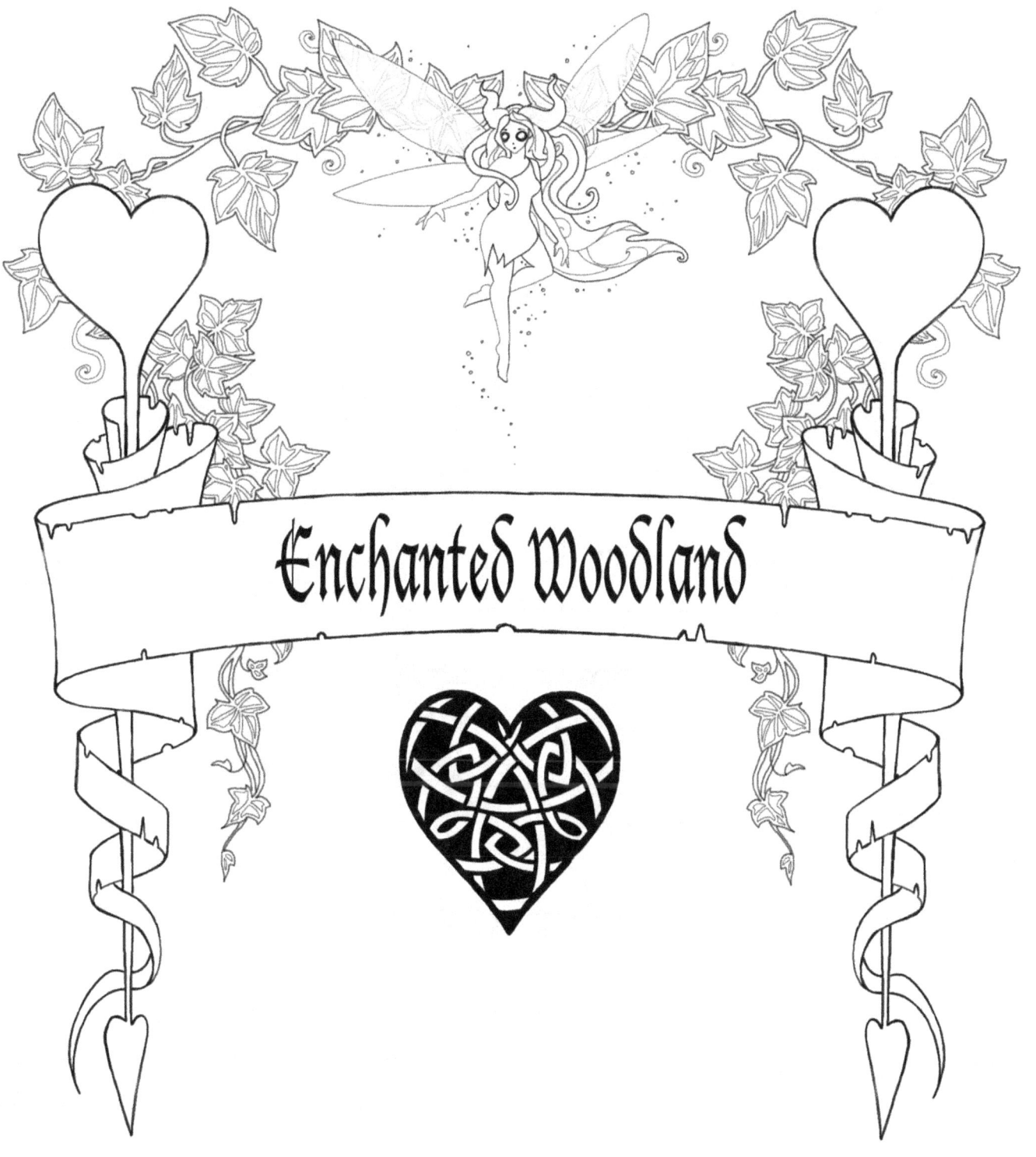

Enchanted Woodland

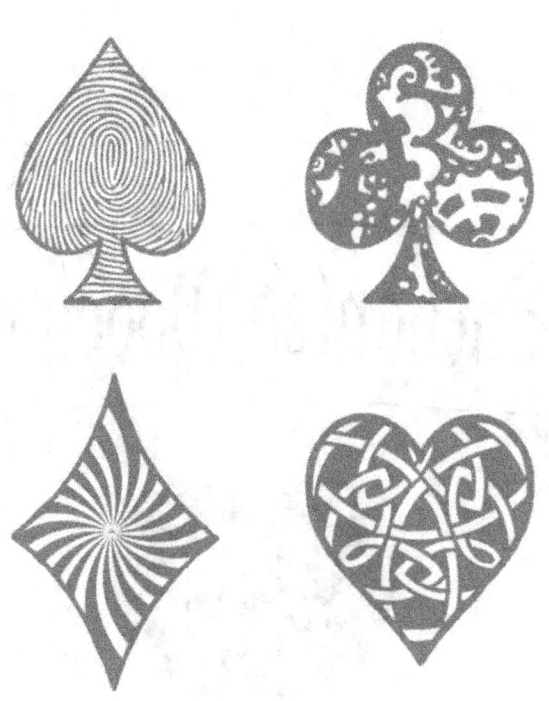

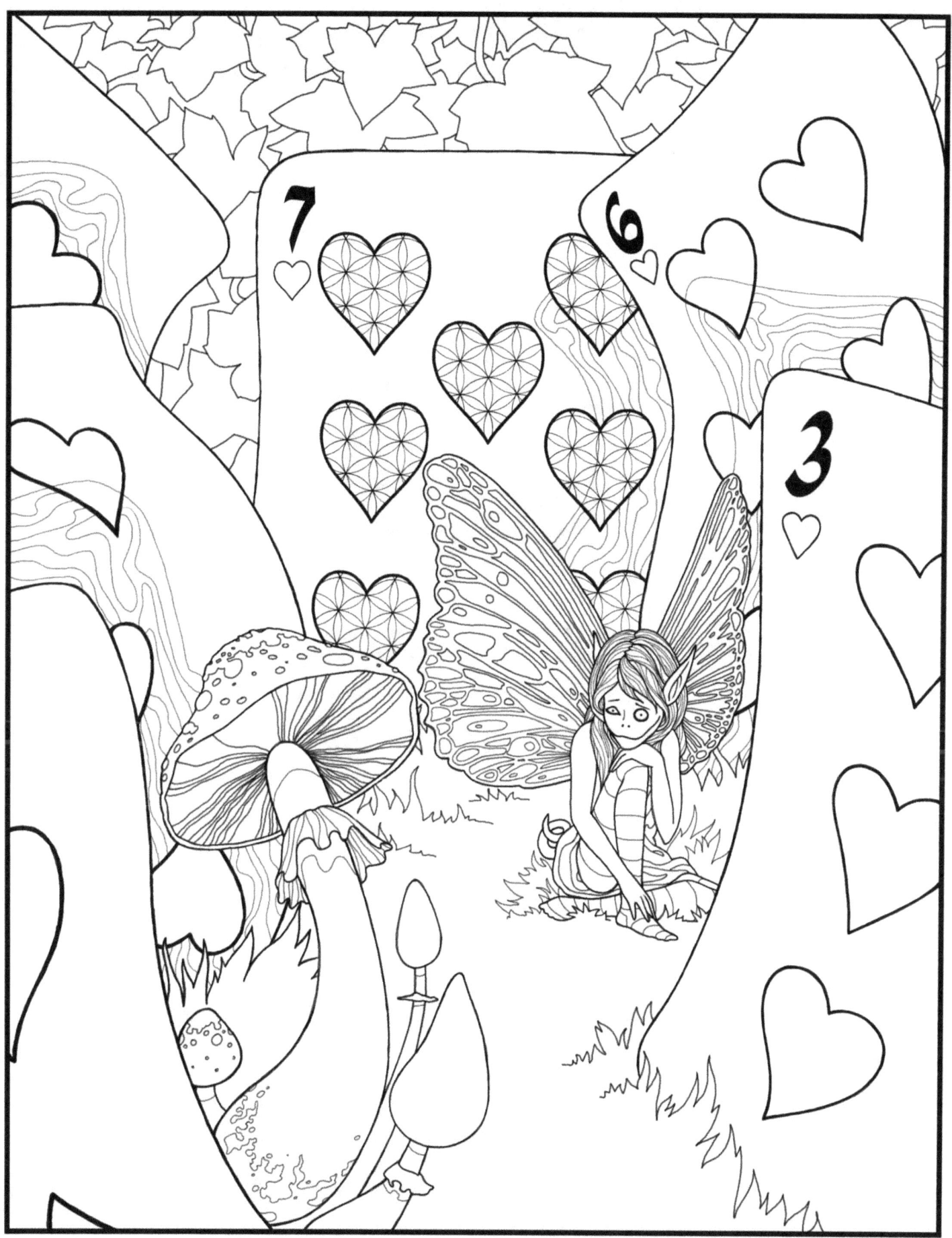

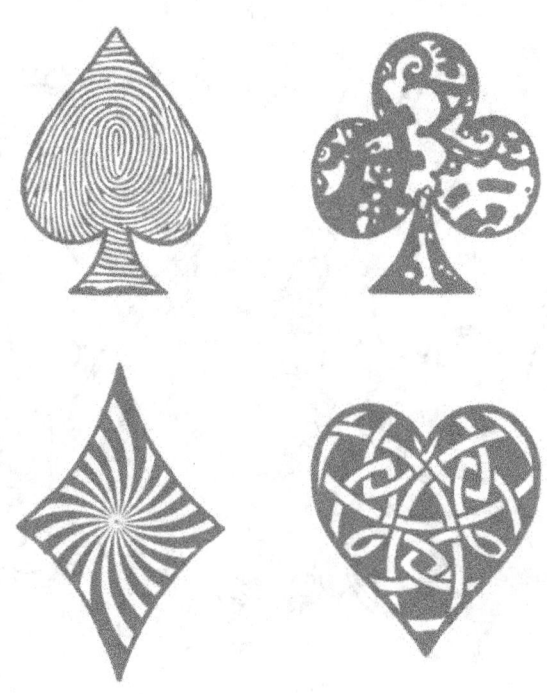

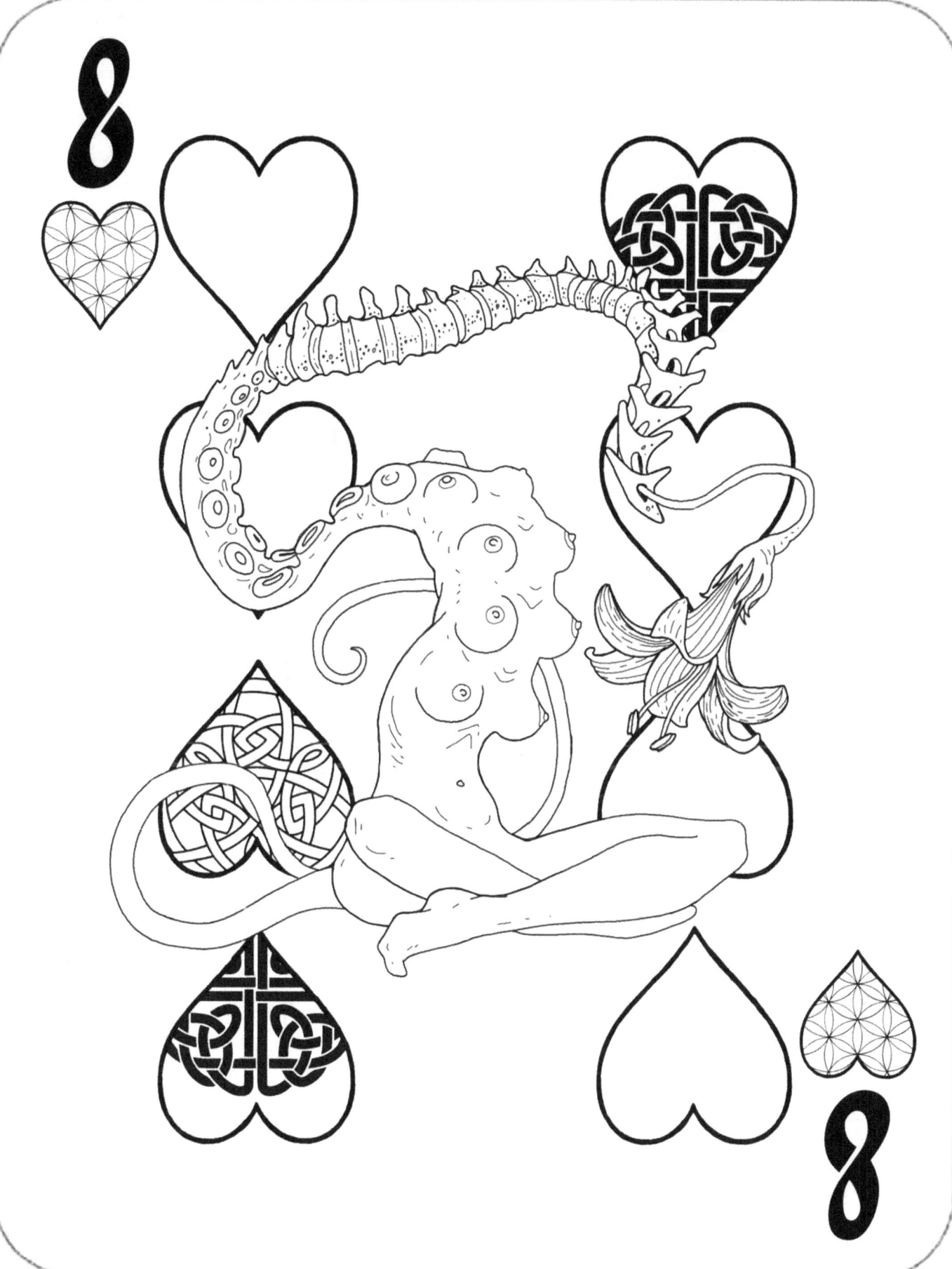

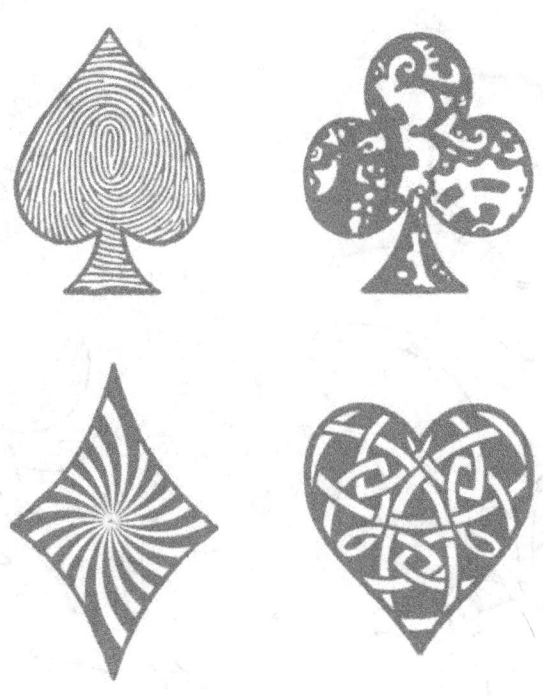

© Lisa Mitrokhin

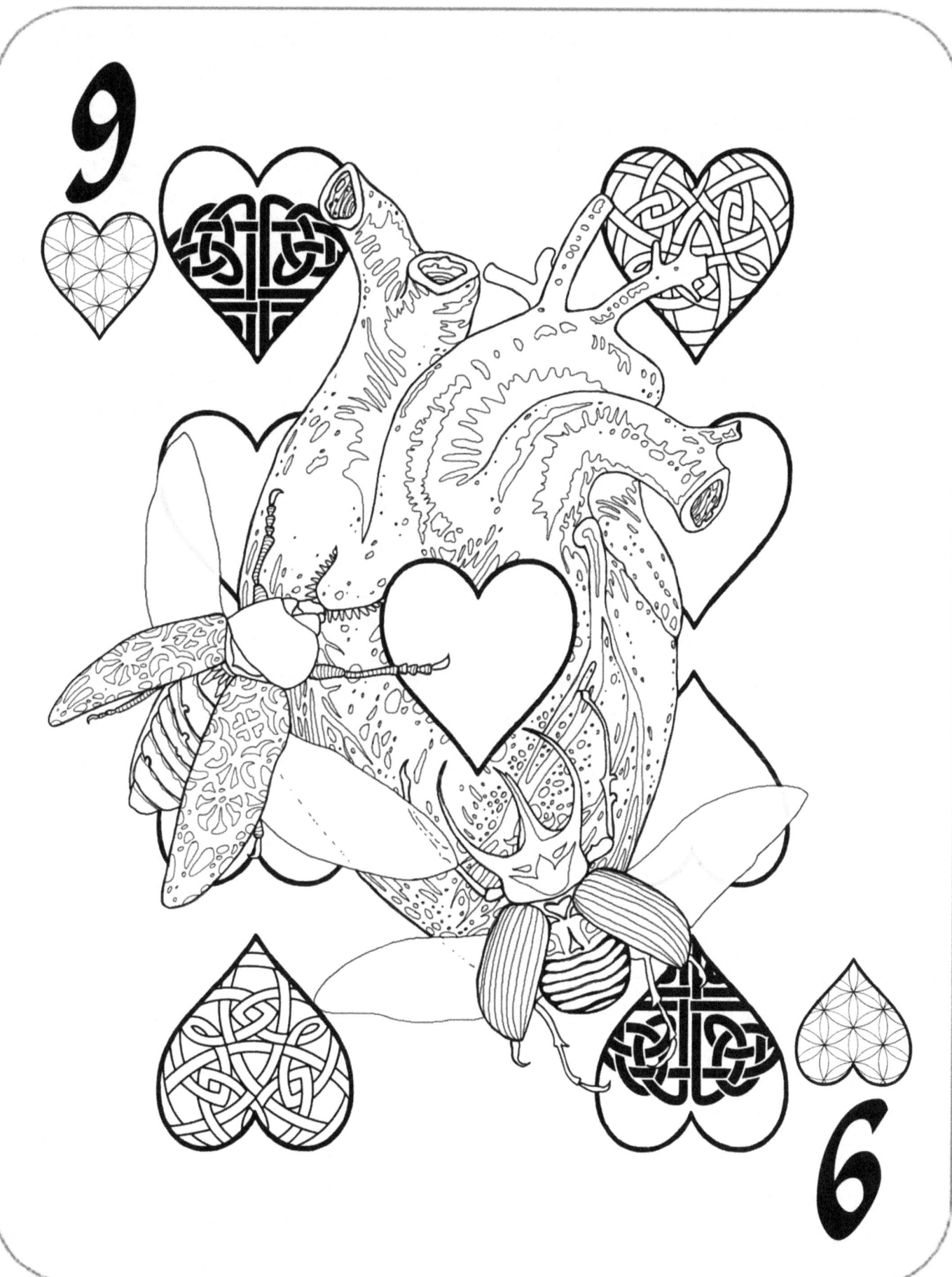

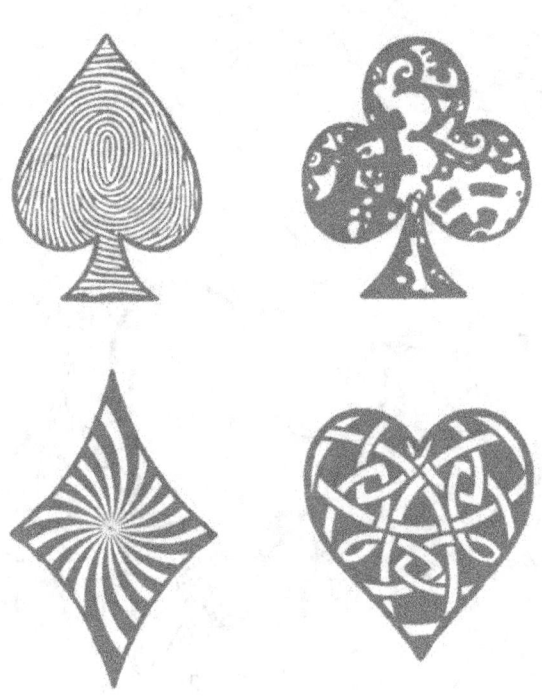

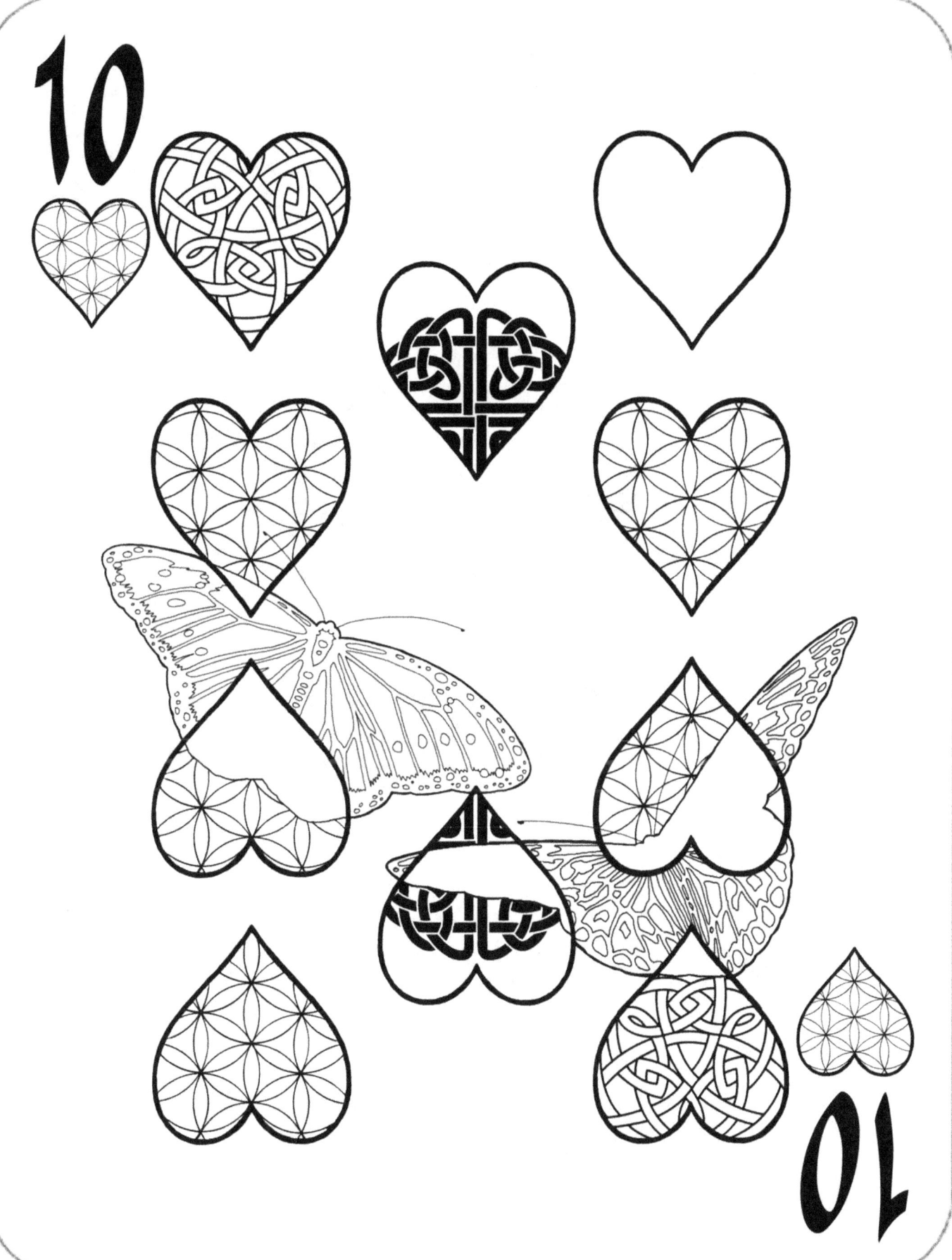

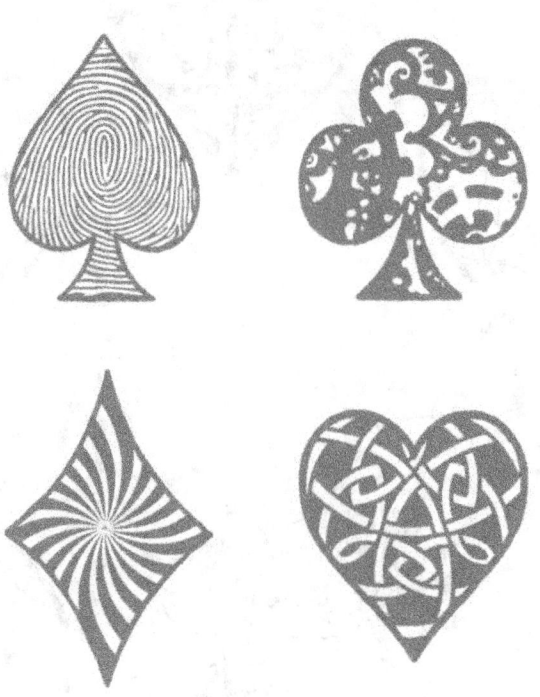

© Lisa Mitrokhin

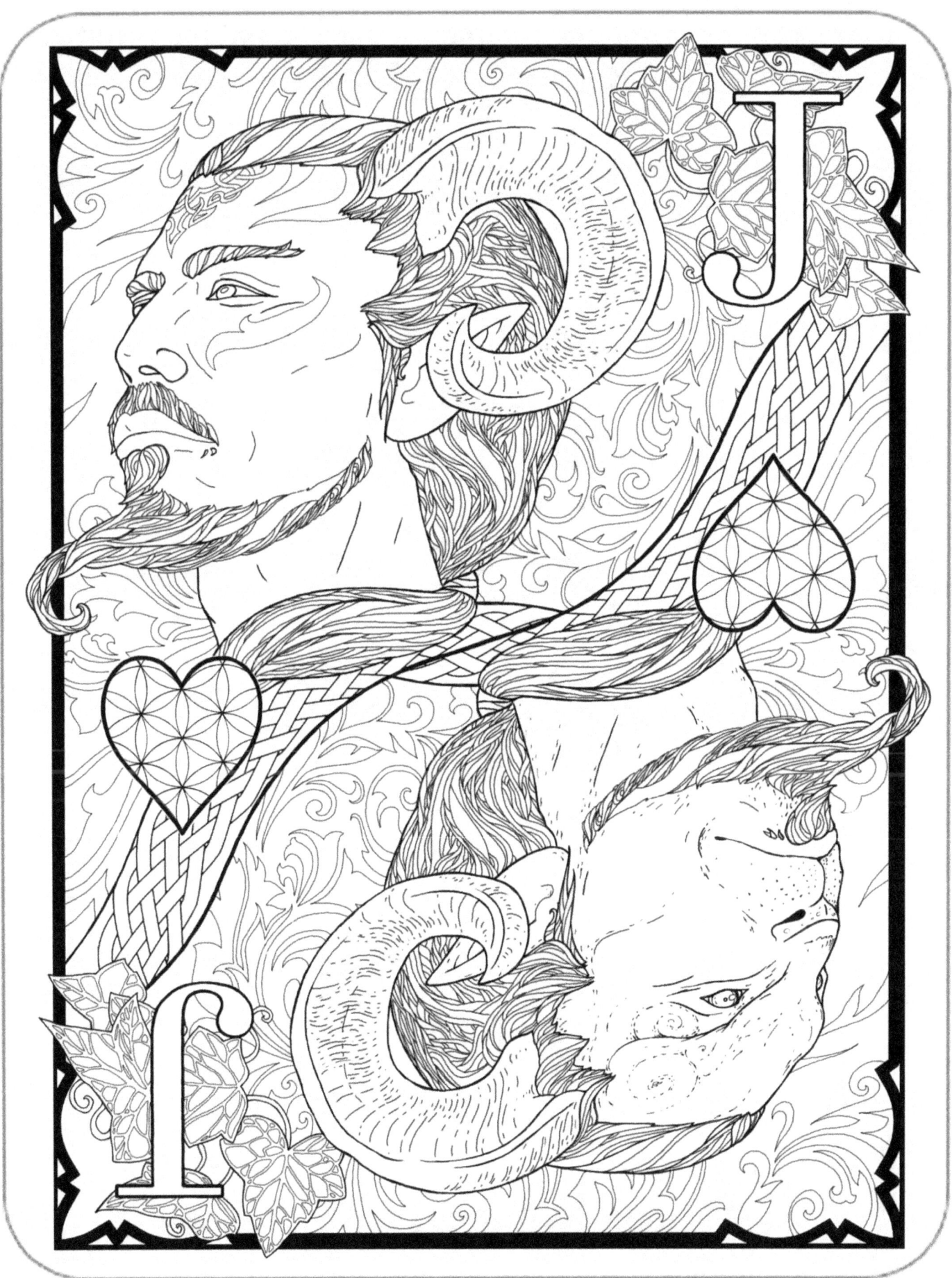

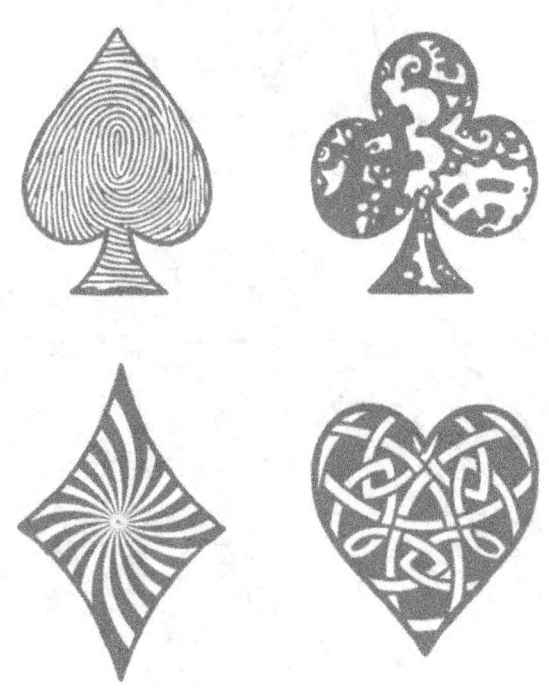

© Lisa Mitrokhin

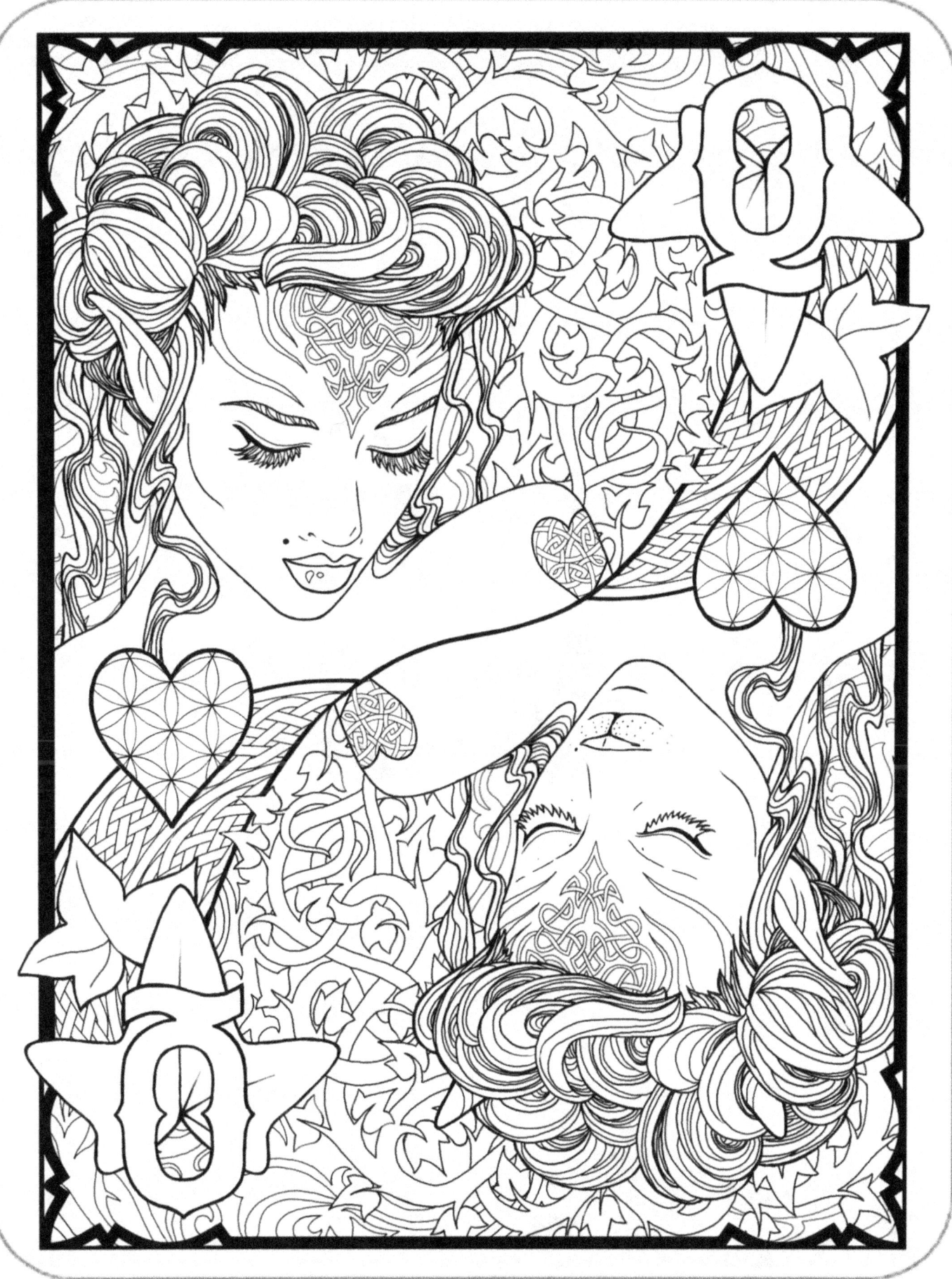

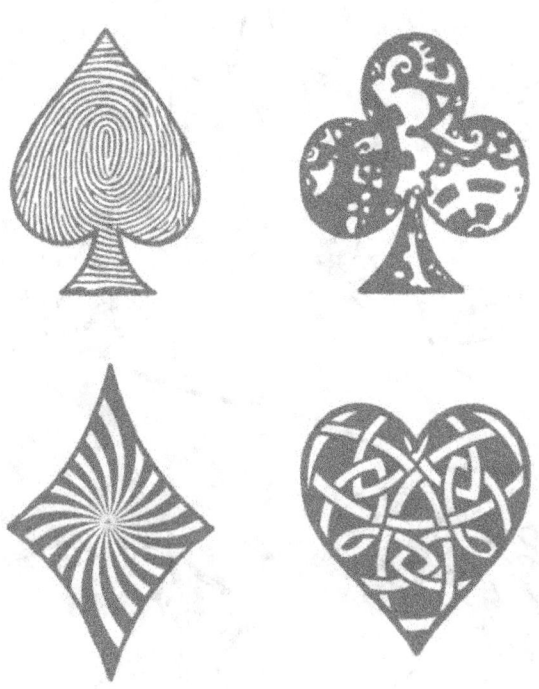

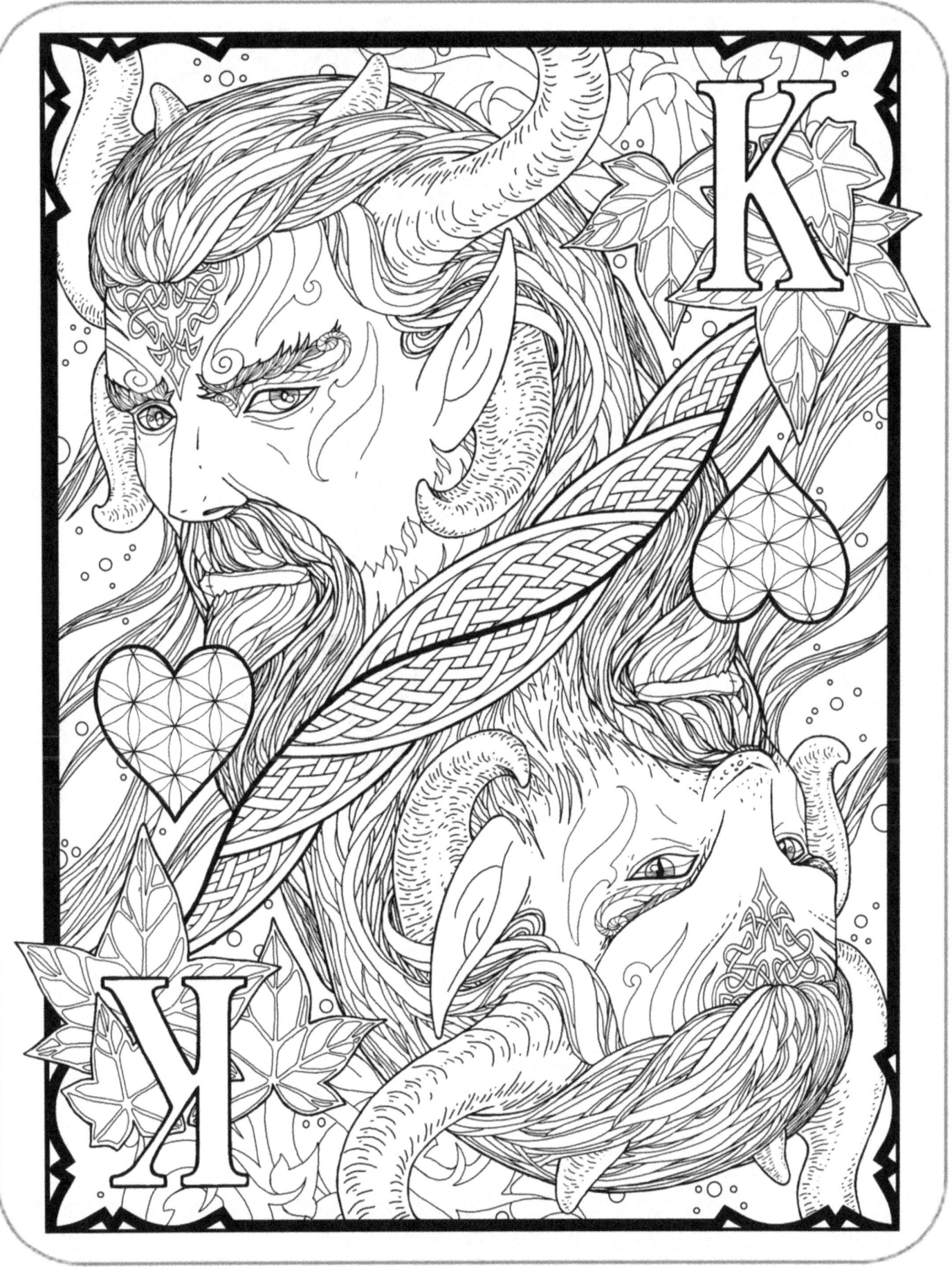

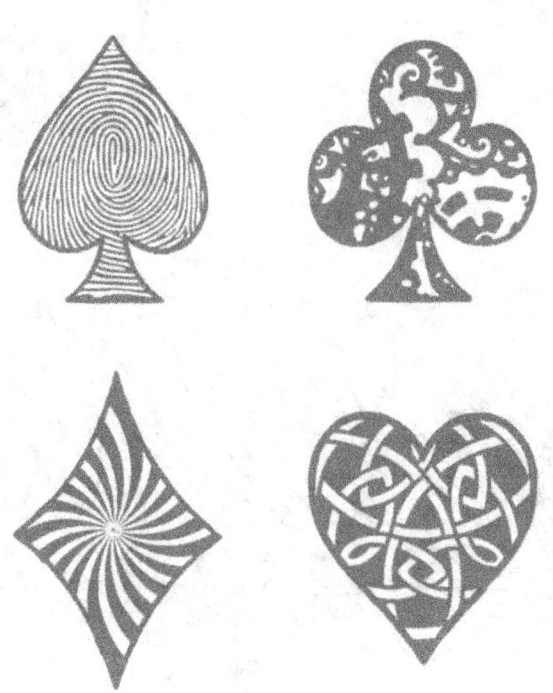

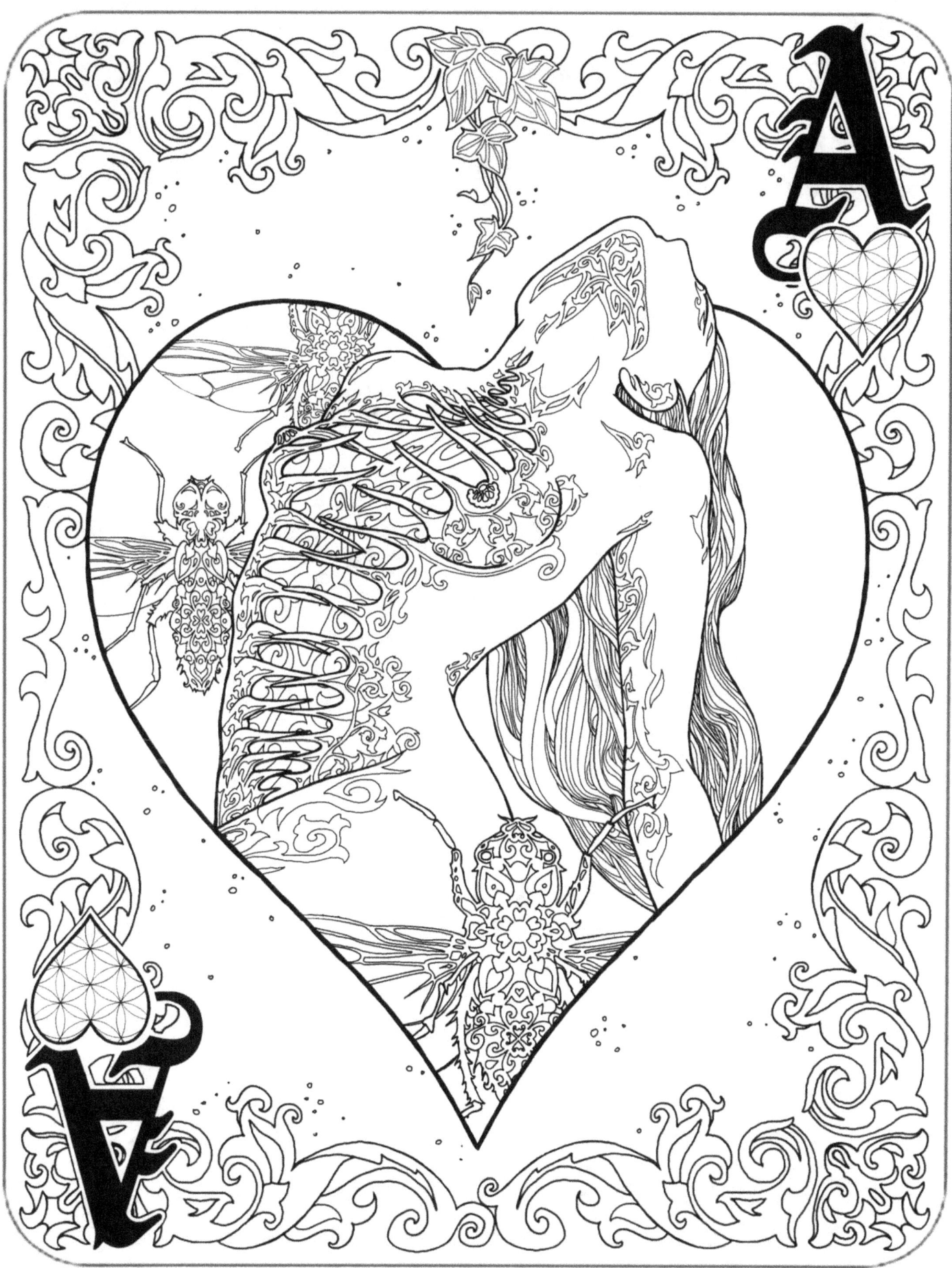

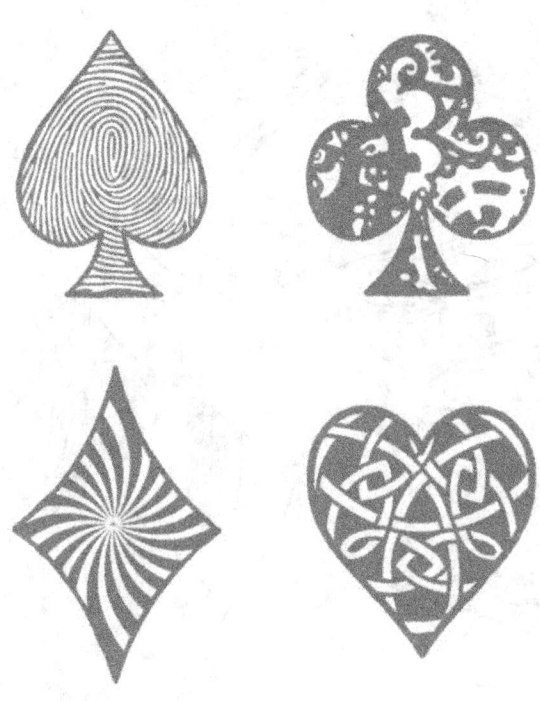

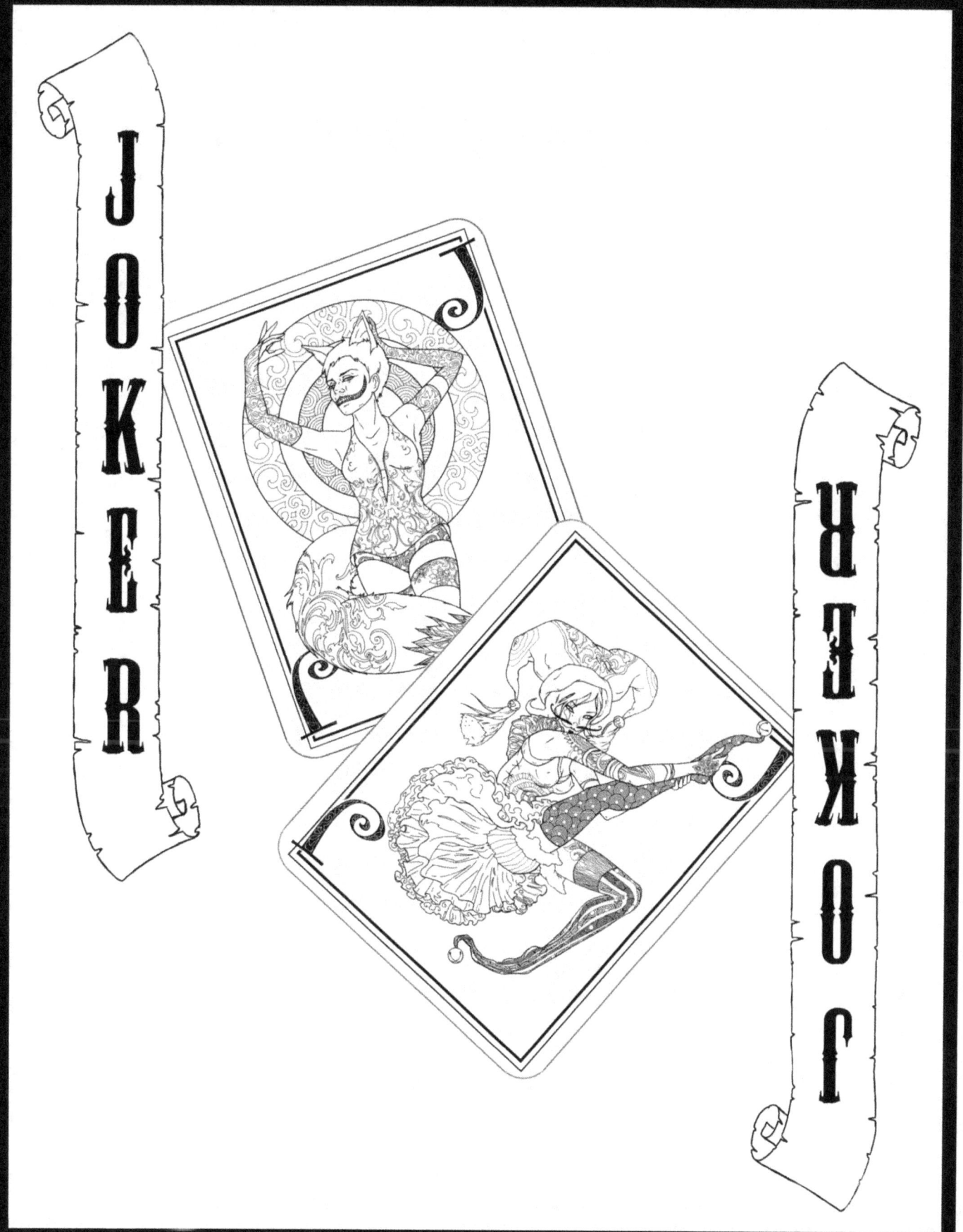

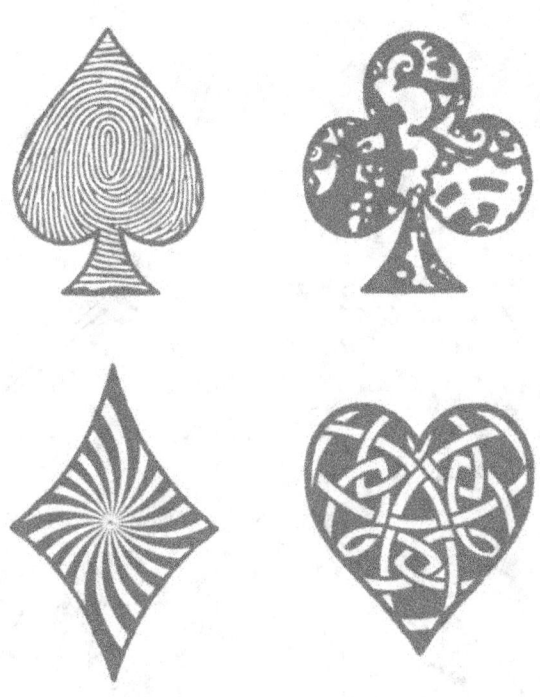

© Lisa Mitrokhin

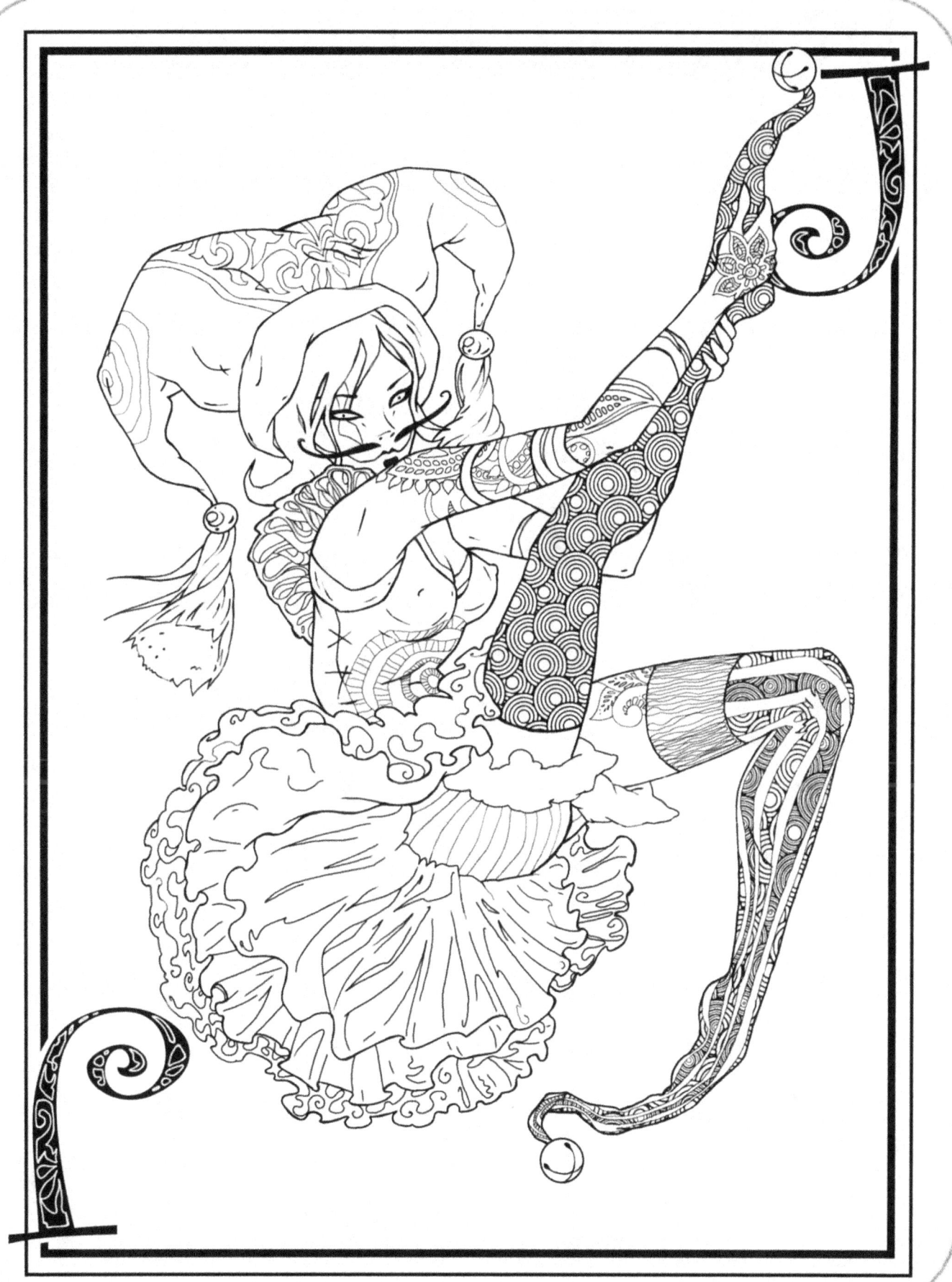

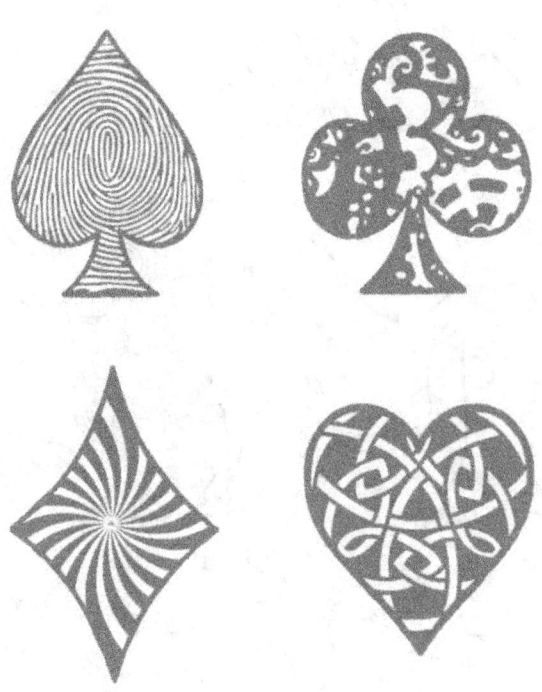

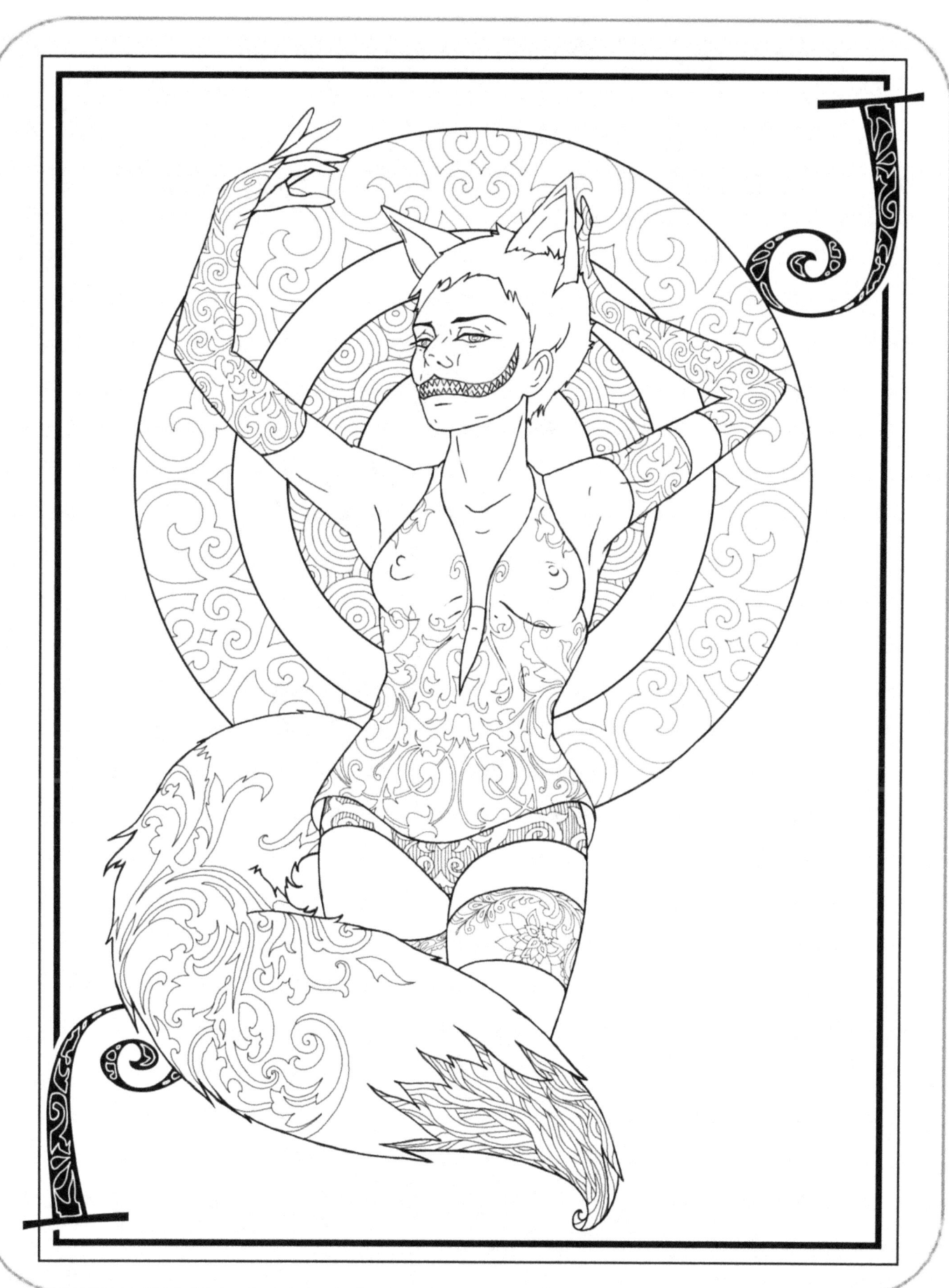

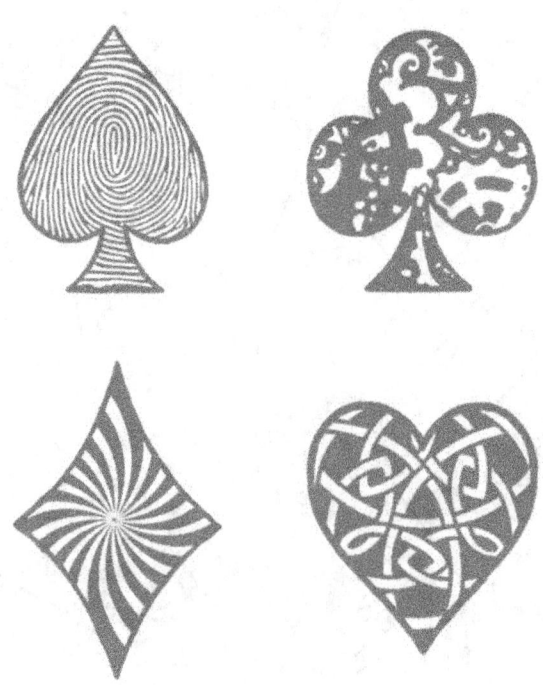

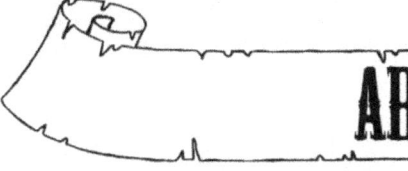

ABOUT THE ARTIST

I remember my first drawing like it was yesterday. I was three years old. It was a drawing of a dog. It must have actually resembled one, because ever since then my parents always made sure that I had paper and pencils to play with. I have been drawing every day of my life since I drew that dog. At first I drew animals, then plants and places. Then I moved on to imaginary creatures. Over time, this grew into entire worlds of fantasy, populated with denizens who have their own stories and relationships with others who live in that world. I have built hundreds of these worlds.

On my journey from three to my mid thirties I picked up a few more media to work with and many new styles and subject matters. Today I work with oil paints on canvas, pens and pencils on paper, digital software, tattoo inks on skin, along with beads, fabrics, feathers, skins and bones on my fantasy dolls and toys. In my creative adventures I discovered that drawing is the fundamental skill needed to advance in any other field of art.

When a friend gave me my first adult coloring book in 2016, I discovered a whole new playground. Being who I am, I was unable to simply color between the lines. Instead I began setting my own characters loose in the pages, making them interact with the line drawings and designs, always telling a story. Soon I felt limited by the provided images and started creating my own coloring pages. Over the next year my individual pages have been shared online in multiple coloring groups. Some are already out there helping cancer survivors cope with pain, some have been auctioned off by dog rescue shelters to raise money for abandoned hounds, and still more are used as therapy in a group home for troubled teens working through gender identity issues.

At first I didn't realize that coloring pages can be so powerful and affect so many people with different motivations, but seeing how coloring brings friends together, helps individuals relax and deal with anxiety or simply have a good time, I decided to create an entirely new universe of characters to share with you. The Four Realms is my first coloring book and I have designed it to take you on a journey through four very different kingdoms. In this book I invite you to follow your imagination and to run free in a fantasy world with no limits.

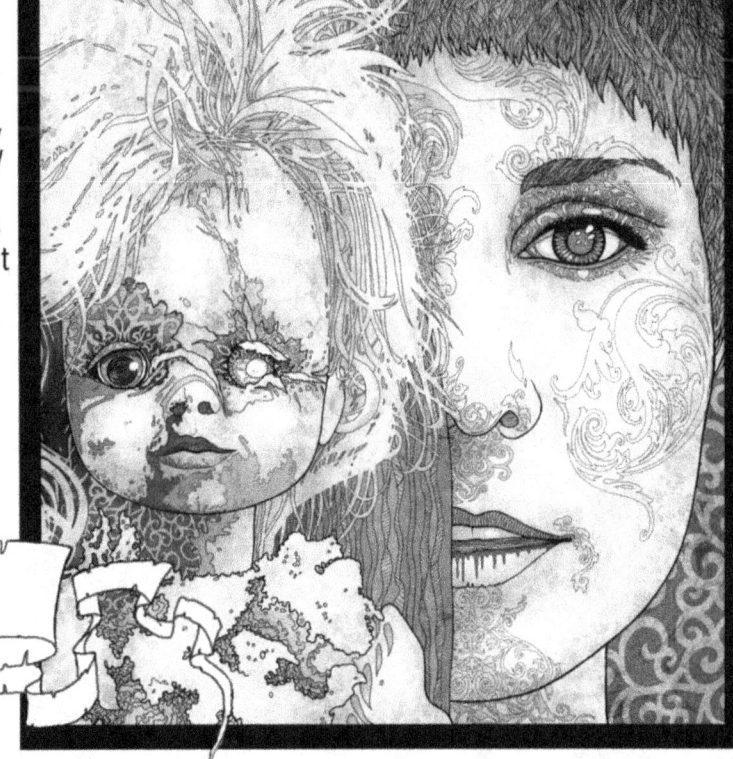

Lisa Mitrokhin

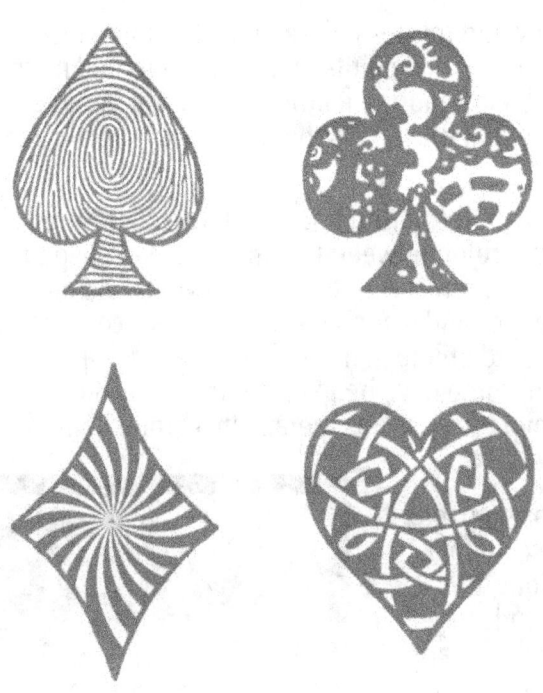